SlowFood

passion for produce

SlowFood
a passion for produce

Jared Ingersoll

Contents

Introduction

Ten years ago I opened a little café called Danks Street Depot, a humble place that was designed to be nothing more than a relaxed space for people to come and enjoy the best local, seasonal and sustainable food we could source. These days, the café is slightly larger but we still keep these slow food philosophies in mind. Every step of the way I have done my absolute best to offer food that is consistent with the core essence of what Danks Street Depot is about: great produce. Without a doubt it is the key to any great meal.

I am a big believer that a cookbook should not dictate what you serve at your table, rather it should give you guidance and inspire you to create dishes that use up the ingredients that you bring home from the markets. Let the seasons dictate what goes on your plate! There are many, many reasons why this is a good idea. Not only does it mean that you will be eating the best and freshest produce or that you will be paying the best price possible for it, but it will also bring such joy to your mealtimes. Even though we lead increasingly busy lives, we should make the time and effort to eat for pleasure.

This book includes some of my favourite recipes from my previous two books, plus recipes that have become Danks Street Depot classics or favourites that I make at home. We decided to group the recipes into chapters related to types of produce and ingredients, to either act as a guide while you are shopping or to help locate recipes that suit the ingredients you've gathered. This book is filled with recipes that will give you the opportunity to learn different cooking techniques, discover different flavours and also offers an insight into how to use the variety of ingredients available from your local grower's markets or garden, butcher and baker. But remember, all the recipes in this book share one all-important ingredient — you, the cook.

Ideally, you should have fun with these recipes. Work at your own pace to make them your own or approach them with reckless abandonment. Be brave and make changes so that you may discover something new and make them your own! I hope they give you as much pleasure as they have given me.

Eat well,

Jared Ingersoll

Bakery

Eggy bread with butter and honey

Serves 6

This recipe is a great example of what can be done when you have very simple and fantastic ingredients, so make the effort to source the best-quality bread and eggs you can lay your hands on. If you can find someone who produces milk and cream locally, you will never take milk for granted ever again.

4 eggs
a pinch of sugar
200 ml (7 fl oz) pouring (whipping) cream
6 thick slices of day-old sourdough bread
4 thick slices cultured butter, to serve
honey, to serve

Put your eggs, sugar and cream in a large bowl and beat together until well combined.

Heat a large non-stick frying pan over medium heat. Working with one piece of bread at a time, soak each slice of sourdough in the egg mixture to coat both sides, then drain slightly. Cook the bread in the pan until golden brown on both sides, about 2 minutes.

Serve a slice of toasted bread on a plate with a slice of butter on top, then let your guests drizzle over as much honey as they like.

Fougasse with onion jam

Makes 12

For the onion jam
1 kg (2 lb 4 oz) red onions, chopped
8 cloves of garlic, chopped
1 tablespoon salt
freshly ground black pepper
200 g (7 oz) soft brown sugar
200 ml (7 fl oz) red wine
100 ml (3½ fl oz) balsamic vinegar

For the fougasse
2 teaspoons dried yeast
400 ml (14 fl oz) lukewarm water
500 g (1 lb 2 oz/4 cups) plain
  (all-purpose) flour
2 teaspoons salt
2 tablespoons extra virgin olive oil
a few sprigs of rosemary

To make the onion jam, put your onion, garlic, salt, pepper, sugar, wine and vinegar in a large saucepan over medium–high heat. Bring to the boil, then reduce the heat to low and simmer for about 1–1½ hours, or until the mixture has stewed right down and become jammy. Remove from the heat and allow to cool slightly, then transfer to a food processor and process until smooth. Pour into sterilised airtight jars and seal when cool. The onion jam can be stored for up to 6 months; refrigerate after opening.

To make the fougasse, put the yeast and water in a bowl and stir until it dissolves, then allow to sit for a couple of minutes.

Combine the flour and the salt together in a large bowl and add the yeast mixture and olive oil. Use your hands to knead until you have a smooth but slightly tacky dough — you may need to add a touch more flour if it is too wet or a little more water if dry. Place into a lightly oiled bowl, cover with plastic wrap and set aside in a warm draught-free place for about 30–40 minutes, or until the dough has doubled in size.

Use your hands to knock back the dough, cover again, and set aside for a further 30–40 minutes until risen. Knock back the dough and knead gently on a lightly floured bench until a soft, smooth dough forms.

Divide the dough into 12 even-sized portions and shape each portion into a bun. Use a rolling pin to roll out each bun into a long oval shape, about as long and wide as your hand. Place on lightly greased baking trays and use a sharp knife to make five slashes in each oval, then open the holes up slightly by lifting and pulling on the dough.

Preheat the oven to 220°C (425°F/Gas 7). Brush each fougasse with a smear of onion jam, sprinkle over the rosemary and then set aside for 20 minutes, or until doubled in size. Bake for 12–13 minutes, or until they are light brown and sound hollow when you tap them.

Pitta bread

Makes 12

This is a great recipe to add to your collection. You can stuff your pittas with anything you fancy for a tasty lunch or picnic idea — one of my all-time favourite fillings is roasted lamb leg with avocado (see page 137).

1 tablespoon dried yeast
115 g (4 oz/⅓ cup) honey
800 ml (28 fl oz) lukewarm water
1.3 kg (3 lb/10½ cups) plain
   (all-purpose) flour
a large pinch of salt
oil, for greasing

Put the yeast, honey and water in a bowl and stir to dissolve the yeast; allow this to sit for about 10 minutes. Sift the flour and salt into a large bowl, make a well in the centre and quickly add the water and yeast mixture. Form into a dough and knead for a couple of moments until the dough is soft and just a little sticky. Lightly oil a clean bowl and place the dough into this bowl, cover with a damp cloth and leave to prove for about 2 hours; it should double in size.

Preheat your oven to 250°C (500°F/Gas 9) (or as hot as it will go). Lightly grease two baking trays and line with baking paper. When you are ready, knock back the dough and divide into 12 even-sized portions. Form each portion into a ball, then, using the heel of your hand, flatten them out into round loaves about 1 cm (½ inch) thick.

Place the pitta breads onto the baking trays and bake for about 4 minutes, then turn over and cook for a further 4 minutes, or until just browned. If you are not serving straight away allow the bread to cool on a wire rack.

Bread sticks with celery salt

3 teaspoons dried yeast
½ tablespoons lukewarm water
600 g (1 lb 5 oz) plain (all-purpose)
   flour
1 teaspoon salt
½ teaspoon freshly ground black
   pepper
60 ml (2 fl oz/¼ cup) olive oil
½ teaspoon celery salt, plus extra
   for dusting
dried celery (optional) (see note)

 You can make your own dried celery by thinly slicing celery stalks. Place them in a single layer on a baking tray and cook in an 80°C (160°F/Gas ¼) oven for at least 2 hours, or until crisp and dry.

Dissolve the yeast in a bowl with the water and stir until it dissolves, then allow to sit for a couple of minutes.

Combine the flour, salt and pepper together in a large bowl and stir in the olive oil and celery salt. Add the yeast mixture and use your hands to knead lightly to make a dough — you may need to add a touch more flour if it is too wet or a little more water if dry. Place into a lightly oiled bowl, cover with plastic wrap and set aside in a warm draught-free place for about 30-40 minutes, or until the dough has doubled in size.

When you are ready, knock back the dough and knead lightly for about 10 minutes, then return to the oiled bowl, cover, and refrigerate for at least 2 hours.

Preheat the oven to 220°C (425°F/Gas 7). Lightly grease two baking trays and line with baking paper. Use a rolling pin to roll the dough out on a lightly floured surface into a large rectangle, about 5 mm (¼ inch) thick. Use a sharp knife to cut the dough into strips, about half the thickness of your little finger. Place the dough strips on the prepared trays and dust with a little extra celery salt and dried celery, if using. Bake in the oven for 15 minutes, or until golden and crisp.

Panzanella

Serves 4

Panzanella is all about using perfectly ripe tomatoes and the best-quality sourdough left to go very stale. I usually start stockpiling my sourdough at the start of spring, taking advantage of the sunshine. I rip the inside of sourdough loaves into bite-sized pieces, spread them out on wire racks and leave them in direct sunshine until they are completely dry (this may take 2–4 days). Only then can they be stored in airtight containers — if you try to store bread that is not completely dry you run the risk of mould appearing and ruining your hoard. For this salad you need an equal volume of tomato to dry bread.

For the tomato dressing
3 large, perfectly ripe ox-heart
  tomatoes, coarsely chopped
2 anchovy fillets
45 ml (1½ fl oz) red wine vinegar
  (a nicely aged vinegar is preferable)
salt and freshly ground black pepper
185 ml (6 fl oz /¾ cup) extra virgin
  olive oil (the best you've got in the
  cupboard)

For the salad
1 large red capsicum (pepper)
1 loaf of dry sourdough bread,
  ripped into bite-sized pieces and
  dried
4 ox-heart tomatoes, chopped
a few basil leaves
a few flat-leaf (Italian) parsley leaves
a few anchovy fillets, sliced
salt and freshly ground black pepper
a chunk of parmesan cheese

To make the tomato dressing, put the tomatoes, anchovies, vinegar, salt and pepper into a blender and purée — you should end up with about 350 ml (12 fl oz) of liquid. When the tomatoes have blended to a juice, strain off all of the solids, then whisk in the oil. Your dressing should be quite thin and not too oily. Taste the dressing and adjust the seasoning and vinegar as required. You'll be using a lot of dressing for each serve so you want the flavour to be generous but not too overpowering — think along the lines of a well-flavoured tomato juice.

To make the salad, roast the capsicum over an open flame until the skin starts to blister and burn evenly all over. You can achieve the same result by placing the capsicum under a really hot grill (broiler). Place in a small bowl, cover with plastic wrap and leave to cool, then peel off the skin, pull off the stem, rip the capsicum in half and scrape out the seeds and membrane. Rinse the flesh under a cold tap; there's no need to dry it.

Place the bread in a large bowl — you want to have an equal volume of bread to tomato. Add most of the dressing, then leave to sit for a minute, or about as long as it takes to pour four glasses of a nice dry Alsatian riesling (my weapon of choice for this dish).

Add your roughly chopped tomato, herbs, torn pieces of capsicum, anchovies, salt and pepper to the bowl. Gently toss the salad together and serve on plates. Splash on the remainder of the dressing and use a vegetable peeler to shave some parmesan cheese over the top.

Pissaladière with smoked salmon

Serves 8

This is a great little dish that I have made again and again in almost the exact same way that it was shown to me by Tony Pappas, years ago at the Bayswater Brasserie in Sydney. It makes a great canapé or starter but can be simply served for lunch.

For the dough
125 ml (4 fl oz/½ cup) olive oil
125 ml (4 fl oz/½ cup) water
2 eggs
500 g (1 lb 2 oz/4 cups) plain
  (all-purpose) flour, sifted
a pinch of salt

For the topping
4 white onions, thinly sliced
80 ml (2½ fl oz/⅓ cup) extra virgin
  olive oil
½ bunch of thyme, leaves picked
salt and freshly ground black pepper
12 anchovy fillets, halved lengthways
18 pitted kalamata olives, halved
a few sprigs of rosemary

To make the dough, put the oil, water and eggs in the bowl of an electric mixer fitted with a dough hook attachment. Add the flour and salt and mix until a dough forms. Cover with plastic wrap and refrigerate for at least 2 hours.

To make the topping, start by putting the onion, olive oil and thyme in a large saucepan over medium heat. Season well with salt and pepper and cook for about 30 minutes, or until the onion has softened. Remove from the heat, allow to cool, and then strain off any excess liquid.

Preheat the oven to 240°C (475°F/Gas 8). Lightly grease two baking trays and line with baking paper. Remove your dough from the refrigerator and bring back to room temperature to make it easier to work with. Divide the dough into two even-sized portions and use a rolling pin to roll out each portion to make a 20 x 22 cm (8 x 8½ inch) rectangle. Place each rectangle onto a prepared tray and prick the dough with a fork to prevent air bubbles forming.

Spread the onion over each rectangle in an even layer. Arrange the anchovy slices over the top to make a lattice pattern. Dot the lattice squares with half an olive or a thyme sprig, alternating to make a neat pattern — this step may seem a bit fiddly but the resulting effect will produce a beautiful looking pastry. If you can't be bothered with appearances, then chop the anchovies, olives and rosemary and spread over the onions. Bake in the oven for 20 minutes, or until dark golden.

For serving
a large handful of salad greens
16 slices of smoked salmon
  (or gravlax, or thinly sliced raw
  salmon)
a squeeze of lemon juice
a drizzle of extra virgin olive oil
chopped flat-leaf (Italian) parsley

To serve, cut each pissaladière into quarters and place some salad greens and salmon on top. Squeeze over a little lemon juice and finish with a drizzle of extra virgin olive oil and some chopped parsley as garnish.

Eaten hot or cold a pissaladière is a French savoury tart that is traditionally cooked with tomatoes and onions, black olives and anchovy fillets. The base for this recipe is incredibly verstaile — you can adapt various toppings as you see fit. Another way I like to eat this dish is to cut a large square of pissaladière, add the toppings as above, and then roll it up in a napkin and eat it on the run!

Stuffed loaf sandwich

Serves 6–8

This sandwich is much like the classic 'pan bagna' without the tuna. It is a great loaf to make for a picnic, as the sandwich is actually prepared the day before and left in the refrigerator. It is also best if it is brought out a couple of hours before eating so it is not completely fridge cold. This recipe is one that you can adapt to suit your own tastes.

1 loaf of rustic white crusty bread
250 g (9 oz/1 cup) mayonnaise (see page 77)
6 hard-boiled eggs, peeled and coarsely chopped
400 g (14 oz) blanched green beans, coarsely chopped
120 g (4¼ oz/¾ cup) pitted kalamata olives, chopped
6 ripe tomatoes, chopped
12 cloves of roasted garlic (see page 42)
3–4 basil leaves, torn
salt and freshly ground black pepper
pesto (see page 232), to serve (optional)

Slice the loaf of bread lengthways down the middle, taking care not to cut all the way through. Using your hands, rip out the soft interior of the loaf making sure you leave the crust intact. Tear the fluffy bread into pieces and place into a large bowl with the mayonnaise, egg, beans, olives, tomatoes, garlic and basil, and mix well to combine, adding more mayonnaise if the mixture is too dry.

Return the stuffing back to the crust and push the crust together to enclose. Cover the loaf snugly in plastic wrap and refrigerate for at least 8 hours so the loaf can set.

When you are ready to serve, take a very sharp knife, cut the loaf into slices as required and serve with a dish of pesto alongside.

Bierocks

For the chicken filling

4 chicken leg quarters

1 large leek

3 cloves of garlic

½ bunch thyme

salt and freshly ground black pepper

80 g (2¾ oz) butter

70 g (2½ oz) plain (all-purpose) flour

260 ml (9¼ fl oz) pouring (whipping) cream

2 tablespoons wholegrain mustard

1 bunch flat-leaf (Italian) parsley, leaves picked

For the dough

1 teaspoon dried yeast

2 tablespoons lukewarm water

375 ml (13 fl oz/1½ cups) lukewarm milk, plus 2½ tablespoons extra

200 g (7 oz) butter, melted

2 eggs, lightly beaten

625 g (1 lb 6 oz/5 cups) plain (all-purpose) flour

110 g (3¾ oz/½ cup) sugar

a pinch of salt

1 egg yolk

To make the chicken filling, put the chicken in a large saucepan with the leek, garlic, thyme and plenty of salt and pepper, cover with water and simmer for 1 hour, or until the chicken is tender. Allow to cool, then strain and reserve the chicken stock — you should have 400 ml (14 fl oz). Remove the meat from the bones, discarding the skin and bones. Finely chop the meat and leek.

Heat the butter in a large heavy-based saucepan over medium heat until it melts. Add the flour and stir for 5 minutes. Add the chicken stock, a little at a time, stirring really well to avoid any lumps forming. Add the cream and the mustard and cook until it comes to the boil, then add the chicken, leek and parsley, and stir well. Set aside to cool.

To make the dough, put the yeast and water in a bowl and stir until it dissolves; allow to sit for a couple of minutes.

Put the milk, butter and eggs in a large bowl and add the yeast mixture, stirring to combine. Put the flour, sugar and salt in a separate bowl then add the milk mixture. Use your hands to knead until you have a smooth but slightly tacky dough — you may need to add a touch more flour if it is too wet or a little more water if dry. Place into a lightly oiled bowl, cover with plastic wrap and set aside in a warm draught-free place for about 30-40 minutes, or until the dough has doubled in size. Knock back the dough, cover again and set aside for a further 30–40 minutes until risen again.

Preheat the oven to 200°C (400°F/Gas 6). Lightly grease two baking trays. Knock back the dough and knead gently for 1–2 minutes on a lightly floured bench. Divide the dough into eight even-sized portions. Use a rolling pin to roll each portion out into a circle with a 25 cm (10 inch) diameter, about 1 cm (½ inch) thick.

Place a spoonful of the chicken filling into the centre of each circle, then pull the dough over and pinch to completely enclose the filling. Place the buns, seam side down, on the trays. Whisk together the egg yolk and extra milk in a bowl, then brush over the top of the buns. Bake in the oven for 16–18 minutes, or until golden brown.

Pretzels with walnut 'butter'

Makes 16

I love pretzels, either straight from the oven or crisp and dried out a few days later. They are a great thing to make with kids, as the dough is very simple and forgiving and you can come up with all sorts of fun and interesting shapes to keep them entertained. Served with spiced walnut butter they really come into their own.

For the pretzels

900 g (2 lb/7¼ cups) plain (all-purpose) flour

60 g (2¼ oz/⅓ cup) soft brown sugar

2 teaspoons salt

1 tablespoon dried yeast

500 ml (17 fl oz/2 cups) warm water

750 ml (26 fl oz/3 cups) boiling water

1 tablespoon bicarbonate of soda (baking soda)

sea salt and sesame seeds, or your favourite sprinkles

To make the pretzels, combine the flour, sugar and salt in a large bowl, then make a well in the centre. In a bowl, mix the yeast with 1–2 tablespoons of the warm water to dissolve the yeast; let it sit for a brief moment. Pour the remaining water into the yeast mixture, then pour this mixture into the well made in your flour. Start combining all of the liquid into your flour until it has just come together, then continue to knead the dough while still in the bowl until it becomes nice and smooth. Cover with a damp cloth and leave to prove in a warm draught-free place for 30 minutes, or until it doubles in size.

Preheat your oven to 230°C (450°F/Gas 8). Lightly grease two baking trays. Knock back the dough and divide it into 16 even pieces, about the size of a golf ball. Use a lightly floured rolling pin to roll it into thin sausage shapes, about 30 cm (12 inches) long.

To shape a pretzel, create a loop with the rolled dough and overlap so that each end has about an 8 cm (3¼ inch) overhang. Twist the dough to seal this join and flip the knot back toward the curve of the loop to form a figure-eight.

In a saucepan, combine the boiling water and bicarbonate of soda, bring back to the boil, then drop your pretzels in the boiling water for about 2 minutes, or until they start to rise to the surface. Remove them from the water and put them straight onto the prepared trays. Sprinkle them with your favourite flavouring, such as sea salt and sesame seeds, then bake in the oven, in batches, for about 12 minutes.

For the walnut 'butter'
400 g (14 oz/4 cups) walnuts
1 teaspoon salt
a pinch of sugar
a pinch of chilli powder, optional
125 ml (4 fl oz/½ cup) walnut oil

The best walnuts for making walnut 'butter' will come from walnuts that you shell yourself in autumn or early winter. You can use pre-shelled walnuts if you prefer, but be warned: once you use fresh walnuts you will never go back!

To make the walnut 'butter', put all of the ingredients in a blender. You can leave out the chilli if you prefer, but I like the gentle heat it adds to the 'butter', making it work well as a savoury spread. Blend the ingredients, taking care to scrape down the side of the blender from time to time. Keep blending until it has formed a paste and from there simply blend until you have the texture you want — smooth or crunchy.

This 'butter' will keep well in the fridge for about 1 month, but you will need to remove it from the fridge to soften before using. As the 'butter' settles, the oil will pool on top, simply stir it back in before you use it, don't pour it off as it will keep the 'butter' nice and moist.

To serve, place a dish of the spiced walnut 'butter' alongside the plate of pretzels so that guests can spread it over themselves.

Salty chocolate cookies

Makes 24

450 g (1 lb) butter, chopped

150 g (5½ oz) caster (superfine) sugar

580 g (1 lb 5 oz) lightly-packed soft brown sugar

4 eggs

2 tablespoons natural vanilla extract

875 g (1 lb 15 oz/7 cups) plain (all-purpose) flour

3 teaspoons baking powder

2 teaspoons bicarbonate of soda (baking soda)

2½ teaspoons salt

600 g (1 lb 5 oz/4 cups) good-quality dark chocolate melts (buttons) (see note)

Preheat the oven to 150°C (300°F/Gas 2). Lightly grease two baking trays and line with baking paper.

Put the butter, caster sugar and brown sugar in the bowl of an electric mixer fitted with a beater attachment and mix until well combined and pale. Add three of the eggs, one at a time, mixing well between each addition, then add the vanilla extract and the remaining egg.

Combine the flour, baking powder, baking soda and salt in a bowl, then add to the butter mixture, mixing well until all the ingredients are evenly incorporated. Add the chocolate and use a spoon to fold through by hand.

Dollop tablespoonfuls of the mixture onto the baking trays leaving room for them to spread and use the back of the spoon to flatten them a little. Bake in the oven for about 14 minutes, or until golden brown.

Remove the cookies from the oven and allow to cool on the trays for 5 minutes, before transferring to a wire rack to cool completely.

 Using good-quality chocolate when cooking this recipe will make all the difference. I prefer to use Callebaut '811' chocolate buttons (melts) with around 53% cocoa solids. They are available from speciality grocery stores.

Doughnuts

Serves 8

700 g (1 lb 9 oz/5⅔ cups) plain
   (all-purpose) flour
1 tablespoon baking powder
½ teaspoon salt
¼ teaspoon ground nutmeg
2 teaspoons ground cinnamon
250 g (9 oz/heaped 1 cup) sugar
250 ml (9 fl oz/1 cup) milk
80 g (2¾ oz) butter, melted
1 egg
vegetable oil, for frying

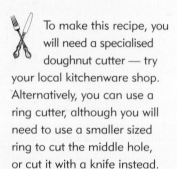 To make this recipe, you
will need a specialised
doughnut cutter — try
your local kitchenware shop.
Alternatively, you can use a
ring cutter, although you will
need to use a smaller sized
ring to cut the middle hole,
or cut it with a knife instead.

Combine the flour, baking powder, salt and nutmeg in a large bowl. Add 1 teaspoon of the cinnamon and 125 g (4½ oz/½ cup) sugar and mix well.

In a large bowl, combine the milk, butter and egg, then stir into the flour mixture until combined. Cover tightly with plastic wrap, then rest in the fridge for about 30 minutes. Combine the remaining sugar and cinnamon in a large bowl.

Take the bowl out of the fridge and turn out the dough onto a lightly floured surface. Using a lightly floured rolling pin, roll out the dough to just over 1 cm (½ inch) thick all over. Using a doughnut cutter, cut out doughnuts or you can simply use ring cutters to cut to the size you want (you'll need to cut out a small hole in the middle of each one).

You now need to deep-fry the doughnuts or you can pan-fry them in a heavy-based frying pan with at least 2 cm (¾ inches) of oil. To deep-fry, take a large saucepan and fill it no higher than one-third full of oil. Heat the oil to 180°C (350°F) and, in batches, carefully lower in your doughnut rings and middles. Turn twice to ensure even cooking and to make sure they are puffy and golden, 1–2 minutes per side. If you are pan-frying, fry them for 1–2 minutes on each side. Lift out of the oil, drain on paper towel, then put into a bowl with the remaining sugar and cinnamon and toss about to coat your doughnuts. Serve as soon as you can.

Brownie

Serves 16

The good thing about this recipe is that this brownie makes a great sweet snack or dessert in its own right or you can use half of this recipe to make the Bourbon and Brownie Fool on pages 56. The brownies can be kept in an airtight container for a couple of weeks.

100 g (3½ oz) unsalted butter, melted

175 g (6 oz/¾ cup) caster (superfine) sugar

2 eggs, lightly beaten

50 g (1¾ oz/heaped ⅓ cup) unsweetened cocoa powder, sifted

80 g (2¾ oz/⅔ cup) plain (all-purpose) flour, sifted

a pinch of salt

175 g (6 oz) good-quality dark chocolate melts (buttons), plus 150 g (5½ oz) melts, melted, extra (see note page 27)

165 g (5¾ oz/1⅔ cups) walnuts, toasted

1 teaspoon natural vanilla extract

Preheat the oven to 180°C (350°F/Gas 4). Lightly grease an 18 cm (7 inch) square baking tin, about 4 cm (1½ in) deep, and line the base and sides with baking paper.

Mix together the butter and sugar. Combine with the eggs, cocoa powder, flour, salt, chocolate melts and walnuts, then mix in the melted chocolate and vanilla extract, stirring well to combine.

Pour the brownie batter into the tin and bake for about 30 minutes, or until it is just set when you shake the pan — the brownie should look a little wet and gooey rather than dry and hard.

Allow to cool in the tin before turning out. Cut into squares to serve.

Bread and butter pudding

Makes 12

This bread and butter pudding is very simple to make, though there are a couple of things to keep in mind: use only croissants that have been made with a really good-quality butter (the ones I use have been made with a Danish cultured butter); also, they have to be stale. The batter may look way too wet before cooking but it does work.

8 eggs

500 g (1 lb 2 oz/2¼ cups) caster (superfine) sugar

600 ml (21 fl oz) pouring (whipping) cream

finely grated zest of 1 lemon

juice of 1 lemon

500 g (1 lb 2 oz) stale croissants and/or pain au chocolat (this is about 5 croissants and 3 pain au chocolat), cut into 1 cm (½ inch) thick slices

a big blob of rhubarb or strawberry jam

a handful of good-quality chocolate melts (buttons) (see note page 27)

Preheat your oven to 190°C (375°F/Gas 5). Grease twelve 375 ml (13 fl oz/1½-cup) ovenproof moulds, then line the base and side with baking paper. Alternatively, if you'd prefer to make a large pudding, grease and line a 4.5 litre (157 fl oz/18-cup) ovenproof dish.

In a large bowl, whisk the eggs and sugar together until pale and creamy. Add the cream, lemon zest and juice and gently whisk until the batter is combined. Add the slices of croissant and pain au chocolat and fold together until well covered. Leave to sit in the bowl for a while (10–15 minutes, or even overnight) to absorb the batter, then fold well one more time.

Pour the batter into the moulds, then top with a dollop of rhubarb jam and a few chocolate melts. Put in the oven — if you're making individual puddings they will take about 15 minutes; if you are making a large one it will take 15–30 minutes.

Summer pudding

Serves 6

This recipe may take you a couple of attempts before you perfect it, but once you do it will become a regular favourite that you can whip out when the berries are deserving of this humble dessert. Yup, that's right, you read correctly, it's not about you or me or the guests you are preparing for — it's all about the berries. The fact is, if you are going to make this dessert you can use frozen berries, or slightly unripe berries and you will get a perfectly acceptable result, but if you really want a truly remarkable summer pudding then you will need to wait until there is a glut of slightly over-ripe berries in peak season, bursting with flavour and sweetness.

1.5 kg (3 lb 5 oz) berries, such as raspberries and strawberries, stems removed and halved if large
200 g (7 oz) sugar
a squeeze of lemon juice
12–18 slices of day-old white bread (you may have bread left over but it is better to have too much than not enough)
thick (double/heavy) cream

You can make this pudding as a large individual dessert or as smaller puddings served in coffee cups — whatever the size you should always serve it with cream!

Put the berries and sugar in a large bowl, add a squeeze of lemon juice and use a spatula or wooden spoon to vigorously mix the berries. Cover with plastic wrap and refrigerate for about 2 hours — the berries will release their juices and become a coarse berry mush swimming in sauciness. Taste the berries and add more sugar and lemon juice if required to ensure you get a good balance of sweet and tart flavours.

Line a pudding mould (basin) with bread in an even layer, so that the bread is slightly overlapping. Spoon the berries and juice into the mould over the bread. Place a few slices of bread over the top and press down so that the bread is soaked in berry goodness. Place a weight, such as a plate and a tin, on top and refrigerate for at least 8 hours, or overnight.

To serve, simply turn the pudding out of the mould and serve spoonfuls with a dollop of thick cream.

Dairy

Welsh rabbit (rarebit)

Serves 4

While there are recipes for English rarebit that use red wine and brown bread and Scotch rarebit that use bread and cheese toasted separately and then put together at the last minute, I have opted for my own variation. This recipe brings back great childhood memories of when I used to sneak cheese by slicing it onto a plate and melting it in the microwave oven and then using toast to scrape it up. It goes without saying I have refined the method a little since then…

a knob of butter
250 g (9 oz) aged cheddar cheese, thinly sliced
2 tablespoons wholegrain mustard
2 teaspoons hot English mustard
80 ml (2½ fl oz/⅓ cup) good English ale
as many thick slices of warm buttered toast as you want

Preheat your oven to 180°C (350°F/Gas 4). Rub a little butter on the bottom of an ovenproof dish or frying pan that is about 15 cm (6 inches) round and 5 cm (2 inches) high.

Arrange a layer of thinly sliced cheddar in the base of the dish. Combine the two mustards together and spread a thin layer over the cheese and then splash in some of your ale. Repeat this process until everything has been used up. Place the dish into the oven and cook until the cheese has melted and bubbles slightly around the edges. Serve straight away as a dip with plenty of hot toast and a glass of ale.

The better the cheddar you use for this recipe the better the result. I prefer Quickes 24-month clothbound cheddar from Devon in England, but you can still get good results with whatever you have on hand.

Potato soup with gorgonzola dolce latte

Serves 4

I owe this recipe to Lynne Tietzel who supplies, educates and inspires me with her wonderful cheeses — it is impossible not to get caught up in her enthusiasm. One thing people may not appreciate about cheese is that like any ingredient it has a point when it is 'ripe' or perfect; depending on the cheese this can take anywhere between 24 hours to 3 years. Once the cheese has reached the point of ripeness it really is a race against time to use it.

1 white onion
1 large all-purpose potato (such as desiree)
a knob of butter
salt and freshly ground black pepper
900 ml (31 fl oz) skim milk
at least 200 g (7 oz) gorgonzola dolce latte cheese
1 bunch of chives, chopped

When you are buying your cheese it will help to know what you are looking for. Gorgonzola dolce latte or gorgonzola dolce is the younger, softer and milder version which is preferable for this soup. Gorgonzola picante is older, sharper and has a stronger flavour.

Peel the onion and potato, then slice separately as thinly as possible — it is important for the texture of the soup. I like to use a mandolin; if you don't have one use a sharp knife.

Put the onion, butter and salt in a heavy-based saucepan with a tight-fitting lid. Add the lid and put on a very gentle heat on the smallest hob — you want to take care to not let anything colour. When the onion has become very soft and juicy, about 13 minutes, add the potato and stir well. Put the lid back on and sweat the potato with the onions. Be careful when cooking the potato as it will stick to the bottom fairly easily. After about 10 minutes the potato should have started to soften; it still needs more cooking, so a little crunch is fine. Add the milk, stir well and bring up to a simmer, only allowing it to simmer for about 5 minutes at which time everything will be well cooked. If it takes longer it doesn't matter too much, but I find that the soup is lighter in texture the less the milk is cooked. Taste your soup for seasoning, then blend really well — a stick blender in the pot is easy or you can pour it into a blender, then pass through a fine sieve. If your soup is too thick it can be thinned down with some more milk.

To serve, put a blob of gorgonzola into each soup bowl and cover with loads of chopped chives. Reheat your soup if needed (but do not re-boil) and, if you have a stick blender, blend your soup well before serving, or you can achieve the same results by using a whisk — you are simply putting a bit of air into your soup. Now, pour your foamy, flavoursome, creamy soup over the cheese and serve immediately.

Sheep's milk labneh with poached leeks

Serves 6

Labneh is about as simple as cheese making can get. I love Meredith sheep's milk yoghurt because it is well balanced and slightly sharp, but that is my preference. Labneh is also a great thing to make when you have too much yoghurt on hand, as once the cheese is formed it can be preserved under oil and flavoured to your liking.

1 kg (2 lb 4 oz) sheep's milk yoghurt
6 leeks, white part only
250 ml (9 fl oz/1 cup) house dressing (see page 280)
125 g (4½ oz/1 cup) olives roasted with rosemary and orange (see page 192)

To make the labneh you need to hang the yoghurt in the refrigerator in a cloth, such an muslin (cheesecloth), with enough space under the cloth for the excess water to drip out. The easiest way to do this is to place the yoghurt in a lined colander, suspended over a large bowl. Refrigerate for 24 hours, then carefully turn the labneh out onto a plate to be sliced, it should still be quite soft and delicate but be firm enough to hold its shape — cut slices using a heated knife.

Blanch the leeks in a saucepan of salted boiling water for about 10–15 minutes, or until very tender. Remove from the water, draining off as much excess water as possible, and cut in half lengthways. Pour over the house dressing while still hot, then cover with plastic wrap and allow to cool to room temperature before serving with slices of the labneh and a spoonful of olives.

Any leftover labneh can be stored in an airtight container, covered in a layer of olive oil. Keep in the refrigerator for up to 2 weeks.

Brie baked in red wine

Serves 6

1 whole round wheel of brie or
  washed rind cheese
½ bunch thyme, leaves picked
freshly ground black pepper
250 ml (9 fl oz/1 cup) red wine

For the roast garlic
cloves of garlic, peeled and
  thickly sliced
olive oil, for drizzling
salt and freshly ground black pepper

Preheat the oven to 200°C (400°F/Gas 6). To make the roast garlic, put the garlic cloves in a large square of foil. Drizzle a little oil over the top and season with salt and pepper. Wrap up the foil to enclose the garlic and seal, then roast in the oven for about 30 minutes, or until the garlic is soft, has nice colour and is aromatic. Set aside.

To bake the brie, place the cheese in a container just big enough to fit snugly, then add the thyme, season with pepper, and pour over the wine. Set aside for at least 2 hours but no longer than 4 hours.

Preheat your oven to 160° (315°F/Gas 2–3). Remove the cheese from the wine and place onto an ovenproof plate or baking tray lined with baking paper. Heat in the oven for as long as it takes for your cheese to warm and become very soft and runny — it's a fine line between deliciously gooey and a puddle on the plate, so err on the side of caution as you can always put your cheese back into the heat if you need to cook a little further, but not so easy to reform an overcooked cheese. Enjoy with thin slices of toasted bread.

Haloumi and tomatoes

Even though haloumi cheese is truly delicious when seared correctly and served immediately, when teamed with perfect tomatoes it will block out everything else as you fall into a delicious world of texture and flavour. I prefer to eat haloumi and tomatoes with close friends or by myself, as strangers find it a little disconcerting as I moan and groan my way through a lunch of this kind.

To do this dish justice you will need to follow your instincts and be prepared, because when the cheese hits the pan it is a race to not only cook the cheese correctly but to also make sure you can get it in your mouth straight away so that you can appreciate the brilliant texture of haloumi.

Without a doubt, it is the tomatoes that are seriously important here — all of the other ingredients are a lot more forgiving, as they can sit in a pantry or in the fridge patiently waiting for a perfectly ripe tomato and so they should. Different species of tomato taste, look and feel different, which may come as a shock to those of you who only ever buy one of the two varieties commonly available from most supermarkets, neither of which are particularly flavoursome.

To find the best tomatoes I suggest you grow them yourself. It may take a couple of seasons to get it right (or you could be like me and be destined for a life of tomato growing disappointment), but watching a tomato grow will give you a greater appreciation for tomatoes in general and help you better understand the ripening process. If you can't grow your own, then go to your local organic market and spend some time getting to know the growers there, build a rapport and ask them for advice — feel, squeeze and smell before buying.

Once you have found your tomatoes and chosen your haloumi (I prefer Cypriot haloumi) you need to get yourself a good grassy and fresh extra virgin olive oil, a lemon for squeezing fresh lemon juice and a little flat-leaf (Italian) parsley, cut into really thin strips for absolutely no other reason other than I really like the way it looks!

To put this dish together you need a hot, but not too hot, frying pan — if the pan is smoking you need to remove it from the heat for a little while. Arrange your tomatoes on a plate and lightly salt them to help bring out their sweetness.

Cut the haloumi into 1 cm (½ inch) thick slices and then lightly oil the pan before sliding in the cheese. Watch the cheese closely, looking for a slightly dark brown on the edges of the cheese for maximum crust and flavour. Once this is achieved, quickly flip the cheese over to cook on the other side (this should only take a minute), then as soon as you have the same colour lift the cheese out of the pan, straight onto the tomatoes. Throw over your parsley, drizzle with extra virgin olive oil, squeeze over some lemon juice and then enjoy it without delay.

'The boys' macaroni and cheese

Serves 4

Everyone has their naughty gastronomic pleasures. I have many, but this is a simple recipe that I love to enjoy in company — in this case, it's my two sons who share my obsession. The ritual in our house requires that we save it for those moments when we are able to eat our food in front of the telly and when Mum doesn't have to concern herself with the lack of greens on the plate or the amount of cheese and butter we are about to consume … so it's generally a night when she is out.

400 g (14 oz) dried macaroni

500 ml (17 fl oz/2 cups) milk

1 white onion, quartered

6 fresh bay leaves

1 teaspoon black peppercorns

1 clove

80 g (2¾ oz) butter, plus extra for cooking

3 tablespoons plain (all-purpose) flour, plus extra for dusting

300 g (10½ oz/2½ cups) grated gruyère cheese

100 g (3½ oz/1 cup) grated parmesan cheese

freshly ground black pepper

40 g (1½ oz/⅓ cup) dry breadcrumbs

ketchup (see page 226), to serve

Cook your macaroni in a large saucepan of salted boiling water until al dente. Drain and set aside.

Place the milk, onion, bay leaves, peppercorns and clove in a clean saucepan over low heat. Allow to infuse for about 20 minutes, then remove from the heat and strain, discarding the onion and spices.

Preheat your oven to 190°C (375°F/Gas 5). Make a cheese sauce by melting the butter in a separate saucepan over medium heat. Add the flour and stir to make a smooth paste, then start adding the milk, a little at a time, stirring constantly so as not to allow any lumps to form. Bring almost to the boil and then start adding the combined cheeses, stirring constantly until they melt and thicken the sauce. When all of the cheese is added, taste for seasoning (this recipe likes a good grind of pepper), then add the macaroni and stir really well. When all the ingredients are well incorporated, pour into a baking dish, cover with a dusting of breadcrumbs and bake for 30 minutes, or until the top is golden. Remove from the oven and set aside to cool (this can be done a day in advance), then refrigerate until cold and set.

To serve, simply cut off a nice thick slice of the macaroni cheese and dust with a little flour. Heat some butter in a large non-stick frying pan over medium–high heat, (be generous with the butter), then carefully place in your macaroni cheese slice, being careful not to disturb it until it has formed a nice golden brown crust around the edges. Turn over to cook the other side, then remove to a plate. I usually serve this with a dollop of ketchup, *Toy Story 3*, a couple of glasses of milk for the boys and a beer for me.

Raw and candied beetroot with goat's cheese

Serves 6

I once received some fantastic beetroots that were delivered to me on the same day as they were picked. They were about the size of my fist and were so juicy they literally bled when I cut into one. I then had a dilemma: do I cook them or do I serve them raw? And being someone who simply hates having to choose, I decided to show them both ways.

For the preparation of the beetroot
6–8 beetroots (beets) with stalks, about 150–175 g (5½–6 oz) each

For the candied beetroot
a splash of olive oil
4 French shallots, finely diced
10 g (¼ oz/1 cup) thinly sliced beetroot stems
1 small red chilli, seeded
salt and freshly ground black pepper
4–5 of your peeled beetroots, diced
300 ml (10½ fl oz) apple liquor or alcoholic cider

For the sliced raw beetroot
the remainder of your peeled beetroots
a drizzle of peppery extra virgin olive oil
salt and freshly ground black pepper

For serving
a splash of olive oil
salt and freshly ground black pepper
about 150 g (5½ oz) soft goat's cheese, sliced
a few sprigs of fresh marjoram

To prepare the beetroots, first wash them well in cold water, including the stems. Cut the stems off at the base and pick through the leaves, choosing the smallest leaves to use as a salad to garnish the final dish. Take about 18 of the best looking stems and slice them as thinly as you can — you will need 10 g (¼ oz/1 cup). Set aside. Peel all the beetroot. Some of these will be cooked and used in the candied beetroot and the others will be sliced and served raw.

To make the candied beetroot, heat a saucepan with the oil over medium heat and start by softening the shallot and beetroot stems, then add the chilli and season well. Add the diced beetroot to the pan, then pour in the liquor. Cook for about 30 minutes until the beetroot has become tender and the liquor has almost completely evaporated. What you want to be left with is tender beetroot with a bit of crunch, surrounded by a sweet reduced syrup.

To prepare the sliced raw beetroot, you need to slice the beetroots as thinly as possible: the easiest way to do this is using a mandolin but you can also use a large sharp knife, taking great care. Arrange the beetroot slices around a platter, then drizzle with oil and season.

In a small bowl, dress the reserved small tender beetroot leaves with a little olive oil, salt and pepper. Arrange the candied beetroots over the raw beetroot slices, scatter with the beetroot leaves and then place pieces of goat's cheese on top. Finish by sprinkling with a little marjoram.

Buffalo mozzarella with broad beans and a chopped lemon sauce

Serves 4

You must use fresh mozzarella for this recipe, and if you are lucky enough to get hold of some that has been imported from Italy, then grab it. I know I am always going on about the importance of using fresh local produce, but there are exceptions and fresh mozzarella from Italy is definitely one of those — it just cannot be beaten.

For the lemon sauce

4 lemons
a pinch of salt
2 cloves of garlic, crushed
a pinch of chilli flakes
6 anchovy fillets, coarsely chopped
300 ml (10½ fl oz) extra virgin olive oil (a rich, peppery one is best here)

The lemon sauce in the recipe is slightly bitter and should be used sparingly. Although this recipe makes a lot more sauce than you need, this is something you'll be glad to have in your fridge — it works well with grilled meats and fish, or even splashed over some spaghetti with loads of freshly grated parmesan and freshly chopped parsley for a super quick pasta dish. This sauce will keep for at least a month in the fridge in an airtight container.

To make the lemon sauce, take each whole lemon and cut into quarters. Remove the seeds. Place the lemon quarters on your chopping board, skin side down. Remove the flesh of the lemon and put to one side, but leave the skin and pith intact. Slice the quarters of lemon skin lengthways into very thin strips. Place your strips of lemon skin into a saucepan and cover with cold water and a pinch of salt. Bring the water to the boil, then drain. Tip your lemon strips onto a tea towel (dish towel) to absorb any excess water — this process will remove some of the bitterness from the lemon skin.

Now return your lemon strips to the saucepan with the crushed garlic, chilli flakes, anchovies and extra virgin olive oil. Place your pan onto a very gentle heat and slowly bring to a simmer; as soon as it simmers, remove from the heat. Now take the lemon flesh and chop coarsely. Add the lemon flesh to your saucepan and bring back to a very gentle simmer, then turn off the heat and leave to cool to room temperature. You don't want to cook the sauce for very long at all, just long enough to ensure that the lemon and garlic soften and the flavours all come together.

For the broad beans

about 1 kg (1 lb 2 oz) fresh broad
  (fava) beans or 350 g (12 oz/
  2 cups) podded broad beans
a pinch of salt

For serving

4 large balls of fresh mozzarella
  cheese
½ bunch of basil
a drizzle of extra virgin olive oil
salt and freshly ground black pepper

If you are using fresh broad beans in their pods, you need to remove the beans from their pods. Once you have done that (or if you are using podded broad beans), you will see that you have a pale green bean; if you remove the skin of the bean, there is a bright green bean under the pale green skin. When the beans are young and tender at the beginning of their season you can eat the bean skin and all. As the season progresses and the beans become larger, you will notice that the skin will become tougher and taste slightly bitter and will need to be removed. To do this, simply bring a saucepan of salted water to a rapid boil. Drop your beans into the water for no more than a moment, remove the beans from the boiling water and plunge them straight into iced water to stop the cooking process. Drain the beans and, using a pinching action, squeeze the beans out of their skins.

To serve this salad, take the mozzarella and tear it into chunks and arrange it onto your plate, then scatter over some of the broad beans and torn basil leaves. Now drizzle over some of your lemon sauce. Drizzle with a little more extra virgin olive oil, then season with salt and plenty of pepper.

Warm goat's cheese salad with chapons and fried rosemary

Serves 4

For the chapons
1 stale loaf of good-quality
    sourdough bread
80–100 ml (2½–3½ fl oz) extra
    virgin olive oil
a dash of red wine vinegar, to taste
2 cloves of garlic, thinly sliced
salt and freshly ground black pepper

For the olive dressing
120 g (4¼ oz) ligurian olives
3 tablespoons honey
1 tablespoon truffle oil
freshly ground black pepper

For the fried rosemary
vegetable oil, for frying
1 stalk of rosemary, leaves only

For the warm goat's cheese
2 tablespoons vegetable oil
6 x 40 g (1½ oz) pieces of fresh
    chèvre (goat's cheese)
plain (all-purpose) flour, for dusting

This chapons are a really great way to use the delicious crust from old sourdough loaves, leaving the inside part of the loaf for your panzanella (page 16) or ribollita (pages 286). You can make the chapons in advance and store them in an airtight container.

Preheat your oven to 120°C (235°F/Gas ½). To make the chapons, I like to cut the bread so as to remove only the crust and as little of the inside loaf as possible, and make pieces from the crust that are about 1 cm (½ inch) wide and 2–3 cm (¾–1¼ inch) long — don't even try to be neat, just start shaving your loaf!

Place your crusts in a large bowl, then add the oil, vinegar and sliced garlic and season well with salt and pepper. Toss everything together, then put onto a baking tray that is large enough that your crusts are spread evenly — don't mound them on top of each other. Now into the oven, which is coolish because you don't want to toast them as much as you want them to get really dry and crispy (dry or really stale bread holds liquids much better than toasted bread). The freshness of your bread and how much oil and vinegar you use will determine your cooking time. As a rule of thumb allow 20 minutes, but check and roughly stir every 5 minutes.

To make the olive dressing, place all of the ingredients in a small saucepan and gently warm through, then set to one side and allow to cool a little.

To make the fried rosemary, heat the oil in a frying pan and fry the rosemary leaves until they start to become golden and crispy. Drain on paper towels, season lightly with salt and set aside.

To make the warm goat's cheese, heat a little oil in a large frying pan over high heat. You want your pan to be nice and hot but not smoking. Lightly dust the cheese with flour and fry until coloured. Flip it over, being careful as the cheese will start to soften, then colour the other side. Working very quickly, lift the warm cheese onto a platter.

To serve, drizzle the olive dressing over the top of the goat's cheese and sprinkle with the fried rosemary. Use your chapons to scoop up the cheese.

Pickled blue cheese and onion salad

Serves 4

While some may say that the very idea of pickling something as perfect as blue cheese is a crime against cheese makers and all that is natural and beautiful in the world, if you can let yourself go long enough to roll with the idea then my guess is you won't regret it. Don't bother trying to pair this dish with a wine, pour a beer instead.

100 ml (3½ fl oz) white vinegar
2 tablespoons salt
80 g (2¾ oz/⅓ cup) sugar
200 g (7 oz) blue cheese
525 g (1 lb 2½ oz) jar of large pickled onions
1 x 2 g leaf of gelatine (gold strength)
2 punnets of baby parsley, trimmed
½ bunch of chervil, picked
extra virgin olive oil, for drizzling

To pickle the cheese, put 100 ml (3½ fl oz) water in a saucepan with the vinegar, salt and sugar. Bring to the boil, stirring until the sugar dissolves, then remove from the heat and allow to cool completely. Pour over the cheese in a shallow dish (the cheese should be in one piece). Set aside at room temperature for 1 hour, or in the fridge for at least 8 hours, but no longer than 4 days.

Meanwhile, take the jar of pickled onions and pour off 100 ml (3½ fl oz) of the pickling liquid into a small saucepan over medium heat. Soften the gelatine in a bowl of cold water, squeeze to remove the excess water and add to the saucepan once the liquid is hot. Stir well until the gelatine is completely dissolved, then transfer to an airtight container and refrigerate for 1 hour, or until set.

To serve, cut six of the pickled onions into rings and place in a large bowl with the parsley, chervil and pieces of the pickled cheese and drizzle over a little olive oil. Use a knife to cut the jelly into rough, small chunks and toss very gently to combine.

Apricot gratin with buffalo yoghurt and raspberry coulis

Serves 8

If you can't find buffalo yoghurt for this dish, then any plain yoghurt will do the trick. The appeal of the buffalo yoghurt is that it has a delicious, almost dry finish to it, and even though it has a fairly high fat content its flavour is clean and light. This is a great dessert for those who don't want to overload on sugar but appreciate a fruity finish to their meal.

For the crumble
60 g (2¼ oz/⅔ cup) walnuts
80 g (2¾ oz/½ cup) pistachio nuts
80 g (2¾ oz/½ cup) blanched
  almonds
80 g (2¾ oz) unsalted butter, chilled
  and chopped
60 g (2¼ oz/½ cup) plain
  (all-purpose) flour
60 g (2¼ oz/⅓ cup) soft brown sugar
a tiny pinch of salt

For the coulis
300 g (10½ oz/2½ cups) frozen
  raspberries
140 g (5 oz/heaped 1 cup) icing
  (confectioners') sugar
lemon juice, to taste

For serving
8 small ripe apricots or 4–6 larger
  ones, or 235 g/8½ oz drained tinned
  apricots
a small tub of buffalo yoghurt

To make the crumble, put the nuts in a food processor and pulse until they are coarsely chopped, then add the butter and pulse once or twice to combine. Scoop this mixture into a bowl, then add the flour, sugar and salt. Using your fingertips, rub everything together until the mixture feels like damp sand. Place the crumble mixture in the fridge until you are ready to use it.

To make the coulis, put the raspberries and icing sugar in a small saucepan over low heat; when the sugar is dissolved and the mixture is just about to simmer, put in a food processor and blend thoroughly. Taste and add lemon juice accordingly — you want just a hint of lemon juice to help cut through the sweetness of the sugar. When completely blended, push through a fine sieve.

To serve, you will need to first prepare the apricots if you are using fresh ones. Bring a saucepan of water to the boil and blanch the apricots for just long enough to see the skins starting to split, then lift them straight out with a slotted spoon and plunge into iced water. When they are completely cool, take out of the water and slip off the skins. Use a small knife to cut them in half around the stone, then make a twisting motion to separate the two halves, using the tip of a knife to dig out the stone.

Place the apricot halves, cut side up, onto a baking tray, take your crumble mix out of the fridge and pack the crumble into each apricot half to create a mound. Place the apricots as far as possible from the heat source under a preheated medium–low grill (broiler) for about 10 minutes, or until the crumble mixture turns golden. Remove from the grill, pour your coulis onto a platter, arrange the apricots on the puddle of coulis, then place spoonfuls of yoghurt next to the fruit.

Bourbon and brownie fool

Serves 4

Even though by strict definition this recipe is not a fool (a fool being a mixture of cream and fruit), it is a pretty accurate way to describe the dish itself and to let you know what you may become if you overindulge in it. I once served these as a canapé at a function and by the end of the night it was easy to tell who the 'bourbon and brownie fools' were. Because the recipe calls for a good bit of bourbon, you might want to let everyone know this when you serve it — after a belly full of food and wine it might be a little too much for some people. If you prefer, you could make this recipe without the rhubarb essence, or use 80 ml (2½ fl oz/⅓ cup) quince syrup from the poached quince recipe on page 246 instead.

For the light rhubarb essence
4 stalks of rhubarb
100 g (3½ oz/½ cup) sugar
a dash of lemon juice

To make the light rhubarb essence, slice your rhubarb very thinly and sprinkle with the sugar and lemon juice. Combine well in a bowl and leave covered in the fridge for at least 2 hours or preferably overnight. When you are ready to cook the rhubarb, add it to a small saucepan along with a little water to help start the cooking process, making sure that you add all the juices that form in the bottom of the bowl. Place the rhubarb over low heat and cook gently for about 25 minutes, or until the rhubarb has cooked to a mush. Pour this into a sieve over a bowl to catch all of the juices, push as much of the juice through as possible and discard the solids.

What you should end up with is a rosy pink, not too sweet rhubarb essence. To intensify the flavours or to make a syrup place this back into your saucepan and cook to the desired result — you should end up with about 60 ml (2 fl oz/¼ cup).

For the fool

half the brownie (see page 30)
300 ml (10½ fl oz) thick (double/
  heavy) cream
60 g (2¼ oz/heaped ¼ cup) sugar
90 ml (3 fl oz) bourbon
a few leaves of mint

Cut your brownie into small bite-sized pieces and place into a large bowl. Pour over the rhubarb essence, let this sit for a few minutes so the brownie soaks up all of the rhubarb and softens.

In a second bowl, whip the cream and sugar together until you have achieved soft peaks. Both these steps can be done in advance and if covered with plastic wrap will sit comfortably in your fridge for a couple of hours. This means it can be done before you sit down to dinner, but the next stage needs to be done as close to serving as possible.

Splash almost all of the bourbon into the chocolate brownie bowl and gently fold just enough to combine. Break the mint into small pieces using your fingers and add to the cream. Using a rubber spatula or your fingers, very gently mix your brownie and cream together until it is only 'just' combined — in fact you get a nicer dessert if it is not properly mixed together. I like to serve this dessert in a glass with a few more pieces of mint scattered over the top. Last of all, splash a tiny bit more bourbon over the top just before it is eaten.

Vanilla panna cotta with fruit

Serves 4

This is my absolute favourite dessert! The simplicity of vanilla, lemon, cream and sugar gives you a flavour foundation that is perfect with any slightly acidic fruit. Tamarillo, quince and rhubarb are all equally good so buy whichever is best and cook it simply to bring out its own distinct flavours. Ideally, you need to prepare the tamarillos the day before you wish to serve the panna cotta.

For the panna cotta

300 ml (10½ fl oz) pouring
  (whipping) cream, plus 100 ml
  (3½ fl oz) extra

1 vanilla bean, split lengthways and
  scraped

the peel from 1 whole lemon, in a
  single strip if possible

1 x 5 g (⅛ oz) leaf gelatine
  (titanium strength)

70 ml (2¼ fl oz) milk

70 g (2½ oz/scant ⅓ cup) caster
  (superfine) sugar

To make the panna cotta, put the cream, vanilla bean and lemon peel in a saucepan over a very low heat and infuse for 10–15 minutes. Don't allow the cream to boil or leave on the heat for any longer than 15 minutes — you do not want to reduce the cream or you will alter the liquid content of the recipe.

Put the gelatine and milk together in a bowl and allow the gelatine to soften in the milk.

Combine the sugar and extra cream using a spatula or wooden spoon, mixing just enough to dissolve the sugar — don't whisk or beat in too much air.

When you have the desired flavour in the infused cream, and your gelatine has softened, then you can combine your ingredients. Add the gelatine and milk mixture to your saucepan of hot cream and stir until the gelatine has dissolved. Then add the creamy sugar mixture and stir to combine. Do not use a whisk or work in too much air. Using a slotted spoon remove the lemon and vanilla, allow the mixture to cool, then pour into four moulds. I use plastic 125 ml (4 fl oz/½ cup) dariole moulds, which is the best thing to use if you wish to turn out your panna cotta — spray them with a little oil so they turn out easily. If you don't have these you can just as easily pour everything into a coffee cup or glass and serve in that. Once in the moulds they need to sit in the fridge overnight.

**For the spiced and poached
  tamarillos**
8 tamarillos
400 g (14 oz/1¾ cups) caster
  (superfine) sugar
600 ml (21 fl oz) water
1 lemon, sliced
1 stick of cinnamon
2 cloves
freshly ground black pepper

If you prefer you can serve this panna cotta with poached quince (see page 246) or baked rhubarb (see page 245) — they all add their own unique flavour and texture and can be used interchangeably to great effect.

Preheat your oven to 120°C (235°F/Gas ½). To make the spiced and poached tamarillos, blanch your tamarillos in boiling water until the skin has just started to split, then cool quickly by running under cold water. When they are cool enough to handle, use the tip of a paring knife to peel away the skin — try not to puncture the flesh.

Make a syrup from the sugar, water, lemon, cinnamon, cloves and pepper by boiling everything together in a saucepan for 10 minutes. Place your peeled tamarillos in an ovenproof dish that is deep enough to take the syrup as well as the fruit. Cover the tamarillos with the boiling syrup, then place a sheet of baking paper over the top to ensure that everything is covered by the liquid. Cook in the oven for about 15 minutes or until the tamarillos are just tender.

Allow everything to cool together. Once cooled, lift your tamarillos out into a container and pour the syrup into a saucepan and reduce by half. Let the syrup cool completely before pouring back over the tamarillos. Allow this to sit for at least 24 hours in the fridge before using; they will also keep perfectly well for a couple of months if stored in a sterilised jar and kept under plenty of liquid.

To serve, carefully turn out the panna cottas onto individual plates and put some of your fruit alongside it. Serve straight away.

Baked ricotta with cherries in a vanilla syrup

Serves 8

This is a simple dessert that can be prepared in advance, then all that is left to do is to serve. It is a good recipe to master as it opens the door to loads of variations — during spring it is great with stone fruits, but in the cooler months try poached tamarillos (see page 61) or citrus fruit. You can also try folding different nuts through the ricotta.

For the baked ricotta

750 g (1 lb 10 oz/3 cups) ricotta cheese
2 eggs
1 vanilla bean
175 g (6 oz/¾ cup) caster (superfine) sugar
200 g (7 oz/1⅓ cups) unsalted pistachio nuts

For the cherries

280 g (10 oz/1¼ cups) sugar
1 lemon
the leftover vanilla bean from the ricotta
100 ml (3½ fl oz) cold water
55 ml (1¾ fl oz) kirsch
250 g (9 oz) cherries

Preheat your oven to 150°C (300°F/Gas 2). To make the baked ricotta, put the ricotta and eggs in a large bowl, then beat together. Carefully split the vanilla bean and scrape the seeds into the ricotta, reserving the bean itself for the syrup. Now add the sugar and pistachios and beat together well.

Life is easier if you use a non-stick loaf (bar) tin, about 21 x 10 x 5 cm (8¼ x 4 x 2 inches), for the ricotta, but if you don't have a non-stick tin, then grease and line the tin with plastic wrap. Spoon the ricotta mixture into the tin and smooth the top, then cover the tin with foil.

You now want to cook the ricotta in a bain-marie, which basically means in a water bath. To do this, place your loaf tin into a larger tin or roasting tray and pour in enough boiling water to come halfway up the outside of the ricotta tin. Bake this for 50 minutes. Remove from the water, take off the foil and allow the ricotta to cool completely in the fridge before turning out — it will need a few hours to cool.

To make the cherries in vanilla syrup, put the sugar, a small piece of lemon zest, the vanilla bean and water in a saucepan and cook over medium heat for about 10 minutes, or until you have a very pale caramel. Remove the pan from the heat and stop the cooking process by carefully adding a squeeze of lemon juice and the kirsch. Allow to cool completely but don't refrigerate — it will take about 45 minutes.

Take your cherries and remove their stems. Working over a bowl, tear the cherries in half to remove the stone. I like the look of the torn untidy pieces of cherry; also you will be squeezing out the juice, which will look great on the plate. Keep in the fridge until you are ready to serve.

To serve, slice the ricotta into even pieces. Remove the lemon zest and vanilla bean from the syrup and pour the syrup over the cherries, then serve the cherries over the cut ricotta.

Fig biscotti with mascarpone cream and dessert wine

Serves 8

I am one of those people who absolutely must finish a meal with something sweet. The beauty of this dessert is that it is very simple to prepare and serve, and it suits those times when everyone may be quite full from the meal but still wants something sweet to nibble. The other great thing is that any leftover biscotti keeps very well in an airtight container.

For the biscotti

500 g (1 lb 2 oz/4 cups) plain (all-purpose) flour
a pinch of salt
½ teaspoon baking powder
165 g (5¾ oz) unsalted butter, at room temperature
200 g (7 oz/scant 1 cup) caster (superfine) sugar
2 eggs
165 g (5¾ oz/1 cup) dried figs, chopped
1 tablespoon honey
1 lemon, zest finely grated
1 orange, zest finely grated
1 extra egg, beaten for egg wash
80 g (2¾ oz/⅓ cup) caster (superfine) sugar, extra

Preheat your oven to 170°C (325°F/Gas 3). To make the biscotti, combine the flour, salt and baking powder in a bowl. In a separate large bowl, cream the butter and sugar by beating with a wooden spoon until it becomes light and fluffy, then beat in the eggs until combined. Add the figs, honey and citrus zest, then beat well. Add the flour and form into a dough with your hands.

Divide the dough in half and, working on a floured surface, shape it into two logs each about 20 cm (8 inches) long. Place them onto a piece of greased baking paper and then lift the paper onto a baking tray. Brush with the beaten egg and sprinkle with the extra sugar.

Bake the logs for about 20 minutes, or until golden. Remove from the oven and cool on a wire rack. When cool, place them onto a chopping board, then slice on an angle into 1 cm (½ inch) thick pieces — you should get about 20 slices from each log. Lay the slices onto a greased baking tray and bake for about 5 minutes, then turn them over and bake for another 5–6 minutes. The biscotti must be golden and completely dry and crispy — if they are still soft they will not store as well. Cool on a wire rack.

For the mascarpone cream

300 g (10½ oz/1⅓ cups)
mascarpone cheese
150 ml (5 fl oz) pouring (whipping)
cream
120 g (4¼ oz/heaped ½ cup) sugar
a touch of mixed grated lemon and
lime zest
a splash of lemon juice

For serving

a bottle of dessert wine

To make the masarpone cream, put all of the ingredients into a bowl and beat everything together with a wooden spoon until light and creamy.

To serve, place the mascarpone cream in a small bowl, then make a well in the middle and pour in some of your favourite dessert wine. Place the bowl on a platter surrounded by the biscotti and take to the table with a serving spoon, the bottle of wine and some little plates, for everyone to help themselves. The idea is to take a biscotti, drizzle over a little extra wine, spoon on some of the mascarpone and enjoy.

Vanilla custard ice cream

Makes 1 litre (35 fl oz/4 cups)

The idea behind this recipe is to demonstrate possibilities. It does require you to have an ice cream machine, but if you don't, I recommend that you put it on your list of things to get because nothing is more fun or delicious than making your own ice cream. I've included a variation for buffalo milk ice cream for you to experiment with as there is quite a difference between milks when you taste them side by side. Buffalo milk has a definite 'weight' and a distinctive natural sweetness. It is also slightly thicker and yellower, and tends to get a little icy when left in the freezer for too long, so it is best eaten sooner rather than later.

500 ml (17 fl oz/2cups) pouring (whipping) cream
250 ml (9 fl oz/1 cup) milk
1 strip of lemon peel, white pith removed
1 vanilla bean, split lengthways
6 egg yolks
125 g (4½ oz) caster (superfine) sugar

To make buffalo milk ice cream, you simply need to adjust the quantities of milk and cream in the vanilla custard ice cream recipe above. Omit adding any cream and add 500 ml (17 fl oz/2 cups) buffalo milk with the vanilla and lemon peel instead. Once the custard has been made, add 250 ml (9 fl oz/ 1 cup) of lightly whipped cream to the cooled custard before churning.

Put 250 ml (9 fl oz/1 cup) of the cream in a saucepan with the milk and lemon zest. Scrape the vanilla seeds into the pan, add the pod, and bring almost to the boil.

Meanwhile, put the egg yolks and sugar into a large bowl and whisk until well combined and pale.

Remove the cream mixture from the heat, pour over the egg yolk mixture and whisk until well combined, then return the saucepan to the heat and cook over a gentle heat until the custard thickens — you will need to stir the custard continuously with a spatula, taking care to scrape the bottom and the edges of the saucepan to ensure that it does not catch. When the custard coats the back of your spoon, remove from the heat and strain into a bowl, discarding the vanilla pod and lemon zest. Set aside to cool, then place in the refrigerator until cold.

Whisk the remaining cream until soft peaks form, then fold through the custard until just combined. Transfer to an ice cream machine and freeze according to the manufacturer's instructions.

Dolce de leche and walnut ice cream

Makes 1.5 litres (52 fl oz/6 cups)

395 g (13¾ oz/1¼ cups) tinned
  sweetened condensed milk
1 litre (35 fl oz/4 cups) vanilla
  custard ice cream (see opposite)
130 g (4¼ oz/1¼ cups) toasted
  walnut halves, broken by hand
  into pieces

Take your tin of condensed milk and place into a saucepan with enough cold water to submerge the tin, then bring to the boil. Reduce the heat to low and simmer the whole tin for 3 hours — you will need to check on the pan regularly and top up with water as needed; there is nothing worse than cleaning the contents of a exploding tin of condensed milk off the walls, roof and floor of your kitchen.

Remove the pan from the heat and let the tin sit in the water until cold — this may take another hour or so. When the tin is cold enough to touch, open the tin and scoop out the milk caramel inside.

Place the vanilla custard ice cream in an ice cream machine and churn according to the manufacturer's instructions, then during the final 2–3 minutes, start to drop in the walnuts and blobs of the caramelized milk mixture, or dolce de leche, and allow it to swirl through the ice cream.

Poultr

Poultry Shop

Salted, spiced and roasted whole duck

Serve 4

The duck benefits greatly from being able to salt for at least 24 hours before cooking. The beauty of this recipe is that it is almost impossible to stuff up; unlike chicken, which can become dry and tough with just the slightest overcooking, duck, with all that delicious juicy fat, is more forgiving. You can alter the spice mix to suit yourself or the seasons.

For the spice mix

1 teaspoon black peppercorns
¼ teaspoon pink peppercorns
¼ teaspoon green peppercorns
4 juniper berries
1 allspice berry
1 bay leaf
3½ teaspoons sea salt or mineral salt
a few sprigs of thyme, leaves only
finely grated zest of 1 lemon
finely grated zest of 1 lime

For the duck

2.25 kg (5 lb) whole duck
as many bintje (yellow finn), kipfler (fingerling) or other waxy potatoes as you like

To make the spice mix, pound together the peppercorns, juniper berries, allspice berry and bay leaf with a mortar and pestle; keep pounding until you have a rough powder. Add the salt and thyme and continue to pound, then add the grated lemon and lime zest and pound some more until all the ingredients are well incorporated.

Take the duck and fold the neck flap under the carcass, then fold the wings under to fully expose the breast. Take the legs and give them a gentle tug (don't pull them off) — this 'opens' the bird up to the heat and flavour. With a sharp knife, lightly score the skin of the breast and leg but don't cut into the meat of the bird; think more along the lines of gently scratching through the skin, which will help the spice mix penetrate the duck. Now, rub the entire duck with the spice mix, being sure to get some inside the cavity as well. Place in a roasting tin to catch the juices that will come off the bird and place in the fridge, uncovered, for at least 24 hours but no longer than 48. Leaving the duck uncovered will allow the skin to dry out, which will give you nice crispy skin.

Preheat your oven to 200°C (400°F/Gas 6) and place your duck on a rack, then into a deep roasting tin. Cook for at least 1½ hours. If you are roasting potatoes, cut them to size and place them under or around the duck after the duck has been on for 40 minutes, basting from time to time with the duck juices. The duck is cooked when clear juices run out when a knife is inserted into the leg joint; don't worry too much if the skin on the breast splits. When the duck is cooked allow it to rest, breast side down, for at least 20 minutes before serving.

To serve, simply take the duck to the table and carve off some breast and leg for each person. Serve with potatoes and, if you like, pour on some of the cooking juices. I like to serve it with pickled and spiced cherries (see page 248) or cured cucumbers (see page 187).

Omelette with goat's cheese and basil

Makes 1

For one plain omelette
3 fresh eggs
salt and freshly ground black pepper
a small knob of butter

For the basil and goat's cheese filling
20 g (¾ oz) fresh chèvre (goat's cheese)
2 large basil leaves

Place your pan over high heat — you don't want the surface of the pan to start smoking, but it will need to be quite hot. Break your eggs into a small bowl and gently whisk with a fork — don't overmix; your eggs should be well incorporated but you should still be able to make out bits of yolks and bits of whites; season.

Add the butter to the pan. It should start foaming but don't let it brown too quickly. Add the egg and, using your fork, stir it briskly in a circular motion until it resembles a very wet scrambled egg, this will happen very quickly, so don't walk away! Using the back of your fork, patch any holes and shape your omelette, then tilt the pan and slide one-third of the omelette up the side of the pan. If you are filling your omelette, add the filling to the middle of the omelette, then fold the bottom third over the filling. Now roll your omelette onto your plate ensuring that the 'seam' is on the bottom. Serve immediately.

For the best results, bring your cheese to room temperature before using. Add the basil and cheese to your omelette just before folding.

If you go to the trouble to 'season' your pan and take good care of it then it will take good care of you. The best omelette pan is a thick, cast-iron pan with an 18 cm (7 inch) diameter, about 3.5 cm (1¼ inch) deep; it also needs to have sloping sides to help shape your omelette. To season your pan you should rub it with a little oil, then sprinkle well with table salt until it has a thin layer of salt on every surface. Place the pan into a very hot oven and leave for about 40 minutes. If your pan doesn't have a heatproof handle, put it on the stove instead. Remove the pan from the heat and, using a thick cloth, brush all of the salt into the sink; it may need a bit of a firm rub. Use a cloth to rub a generous amount of oil into the pan and then put it back into the oven for about 10–15 minutes. Take the pan out of the oven and use a clean cloth dipped into a little clean oil to give your pan a really good rub down. Your pan is now seasoned and you should avoid getting it wet — after you use your pan, simply wipe it clean with a dry cloth. Your first omelette may stick a little — don't panic, you shouldn't have any worries after that.

Caper and egg dressing

Serves 6–8

6 hard-boiled eggs, removed from
  their shells and chopped
3 tablespoons salted capers, rinsed
  and chopped
3 tablespoons chopped flat-leaf
  (Italian) parsley
a squeeze of lemon juice
90 g (3¼ oz/⅓ cup) mayonnaise
  (page 75) or enough to bind
salt and freshly ground black pepper
chopped herbs, optional

Combine all the ingredients in a bowl and taste for seasoning.
I like to leave my dressing fairly chunky and for it to have a good
lemony bite. Add other herbs if you wish.

This caper and egg dressing is excellent served with a
whole poached salmon (see page 169).

Poached eggs

Makes 4

4 fresh eggs
1 part white vinegar to 15 parts
  water
salt and freshly ground black pepper

Use a saucepan at least 10–15 cm (4–6 inches) deep.
Almost fill the pan with water, then add the vinegar. Bring the
water to the boil, then turn down so it's not quite simmering,
only just moving. If the water is boiling it will knock your egg
around a little too much; if the water is too cool it will take
too long to cook and your whites may become rubbery.

Break your egg into a ramekin or a teacup, then gently
lower it into the water and pour in your egg, this way you
ensure that the egg keeps its shape. Don't overcrowd your
pan; if you are cooking a lot of eggs it may be better to cook
in batches, or use two pans. Lift the egg out of the water
with a slotted spoon and press gently with your finger; this
is the best way to feel how cooked your egg is. As a guide,
a soft poached egg (cooked whites and runny yolk) will take
3–4 minutes, a hard egg (completely firm yolk) will take
about 7 minutes. Using a slotted spoon, gently lift your egg
onto a clean dry cloth to drain (it's just been sitting in a lot of
water, remember), season with a little salt and pepper, then
serve as soon as possible.

Chicken stock

Makes about 2 litres (70 fl oz/8 cups)

3 kg (6 lb 12 oz) fresh chicken
  bones, rinsed of blood
4 large carrots, peeled but left
  whole
2 stalks of celery
1 onion, peeled but left whole
1 leek, rinsed
1 clove of garlic, peeled but left
  whole
1 bay leaf
5 peppercorns
1 bunch of thyme
1 bunch of parsley

Put the bones in a stockpot and pour in enough cold water to cover them by 4 cm (1½ inches). Bring up to the simmer and remove the grey foamy scum, but leave the fat on. Add the carrots, celery, onion, leek, garlic, bay leaf and peppercorns. Very gently simmer for 6 hours being sure that the temperature doesn't change under the pot — this is crucial to avoid cloudiness and discolouring. You may need to add more water during cooking to keep the bones covered. During the last hour of cooking add the thyme and parsley. When you are happy with your stock, remove the solids and strain the stock into a container. Leave to cool completely in the fridge, then remove the fat when it forms a solid. Good stock like this one should be gelatinous. Use within a couple of days or freeze for up to 2 months.

Duck stock

Makes about 1 litre (35 fl oz/4 cups)

1.5 kg (3 lb 5 oz) duck bones, wings
  and necks (these don't need to be
  rinsed)
3 carrots, sliced lengthways
1 onion, halved
1 leek, sliced lengthways and rinsed
2 cloves of garlic, peeled but left
  whole
if you have any, add mushroom
  trimmings, tomato peel or seeds
salt and freshly ground black pepper

Preheat your oven to 200°C (400°F/Gas 6). Roast the duck bones in a roasting tin until they become a deep brown colour, about 2½ hours. Transfer the bones to a stockpot, tip most of the fat off the roasting tin and then add everything else to the tin. Return the tin to the oven and roast until the vegetables are a nice brown colour and there is a delicious roast vegetable aroma, about another hour. Transfer the vegetables to the pot and cover everything with water. Place over high heat and bring to a simmer as quickly as you can, but be sure not to let the stock boil or the fat will be boiled into the stock, which will result in a murky-looking and flabby-tasting broth. Cook for about 8 hours. Taste for seasoning, skim off the fat and strain into a clean saucepan and reduce by about one-third. Use the stock within 2 days or freeze for up to 2 months.

Clarified duck fat

Makes 450 g (1 lb)

1 kg (2 lb 4 oz) duck fat and any
  skin you have retained
200 ml (7 fl oz) water

A word of warning before you begin. Because you will be boiling fat use extreme caution — one golden rule is to only fill your pot halfway to minimise any fat boiling over the side. Place the fat and water in a large, heavy-based saucepan over high heat. Boil hard, stirring from time to time. After about 20 minutes you need to start watching your fat — it should be a milky, bubbling mass. As the water evaporates the fat will start to become clear and after 35–45 minutes the fat will become completely clear and golden. Remove from the heat and pass through a fine sieve.

Stored in an airtight container your fat should keep for at least a couple of months in the fridge, even longer in the freezer. You will need to adjust the quantities and timing of this recipe depending on how much fat you have on hand.

Clarified duck fat is used to make the duck rillettes (see page 103).

Mayonnaise

Makes 250 g (9 oz/1 cup)

1 egg yolk
1 tablespoon white wine vinegar
1 tablespoon dijon mustard
salt and freshly ground black pepper
200 ml (7 fl oz) vegetable oil

Place all the ingredients, except for the oil, in a food processor. Start blending; when the egg yolk starts to become pale, slowly drizzle in the oil to allow the mayonnaise to emulsify. You want it to have the consistency of pouring cream — to achieve this you may need to thin out with a little hot water. Keeps for up to 1 week in the fridge.

Chicken and rice soup

serves 6–8

The idea behind many of the recipes in this book is to open up your mind to the fantastic potential of many kitchens' most under-utilised ingredient — leftovers. As well as creating a delicious soup to be served with sourdough bread, the flavoursome bones can be turned into liquid gold by making a fabulous chicken stock (see page 76).

1 boiling chicken (see note)

2 large carrots, peeled and left
  whole

1 stalk of celery

½ onion

6 garlic cloves, peeled

220 g (7¾ oz/1 cup) arborio rice

2 litres (70 fl oz/8 cups) chicken
  stock (see page 74)

4 ripe tomatoes, chopped

1 bunch oregano, leaves picked

80 ml (2½ fl oz/⅓ cup) extra virgin
  olive oil, plus extra, to serve

salt and freshly ground black pepper

Boiling chickens are old birds that have seen their days laying eggs. They are tougher, but much more flavoursome than roasting chooks, making them perfect for this dish. If you can't get a boiler, use an ordinary chicken instead. Of course, the result will be all the better for sourcing a fresh bio-dynamic or organic bird.

Put the chicken, carrots, celery, onion, 4 of the garlic cloves, the rice and the stock in a large saucepan or stockpot. Top it up with more stock or water to ensure the chicken is covered, then place over high heat until it comes to a simmer. As soon as it simmers, reduce the heat to low and cook gently for about 2 hours, or until the chicken meat is very soft and tender. During cooking, gently stir the soup to ensure the rice does not stick to the bottom of the pan. Add more water or stock during the cooking time if needed.

Meanwhile, put the tomato, oregano leaves, the remaining 2 garlic cloves and the olive oil in a food processor and blend to a pulp. Set aside.

When the chicken is ready, remove the pan from the heat and carefully remove the chicken from the soup with the vegetables, discarding the celery and onion. Dice the carrots and, when the chicken is cool enough to handle, tear the meat into small pieces, discarding the skin and bones. Return the carrot and chicken meat to the soup.

When you are ready to serve, bring the soup back to the boil and stir in the tomato mixture at the very end. Taste for salt and pepper, divide into large bowls, drizzle with a little extra olive oil if you wish.

Roasted chicken, corn and stuffing sandwich

Serves 6

The popularity of something like this sandwich really humbles a chef — we can spend a lifetime trying to create the next most talked about recipe and then a simple chicken sandwich steals the limelight. If you buy an organic chicken or a reputable free-range chicken the little extra money will produce a great deal more pleasure. Now, before you start thinking 'that's a lot of work for a sandwich' why not double this recipe and serve roasted chicken with roasted corn and stuffing. Bake a couple of potatoes and wilt down some spinach for a wonderful dinner, then you have everything on hand for scrumptious chicken sandwiches tomorrow!

For the stuffing

50 g (1¾ oz) butter

½ an onion, finely diced

2 cloves of garlic, crushed

1 bunch of thyme, leaves only,
   finely chopped

¼ loaf (approximately 300 g/
   10½ oz) of stale, good-quality
   sourdough bread, crumbed (see
   note page 297)

2 eggs

salt and freshly ground black pepper

For the roasted corn

1 tablespoon extra virgin olive oil

50 g (1¾ oz) butter

4 ears of corn, husks removed,
   kernels cut off with a sharp knife

1 clove of garlic, crushed

a few sprigs of thyme, leaves only

salt and freshly ground black pepper

To make the stuffing, heat the butter in a frying pan and sauté the onion and garlic. Add the thyme and, when soft, mix in the breadcrumbs. Allow to cool, then while still in the pan, mix in the eggs, salt and pepper. Set aside.

Preheat your oven to 180°C (350°F/Gas 4). To make the roasted corn, heat the oil in a frying pan over a medium heat, then add the butter so it starts to melt, then add the corn kernels, garlic, thyme, salt and pepper. Toss about until all well coated, put onto a roasting tray and and bake in the oven for 10 minutes, or until golden. Set aside to cool.

For the roast chicken

1.4 kg (3 lb 2 oz) good-quality
  whole chicken
a knob of butter
salt and freshly ground black pepper
about 185 g (6½ oz/¾ cup)
  mayonnaise (see page 77)

For the sandwich

2 big handfuls of rocket (arugula)
45 ml (1½ fl oz) red wine dressing
  (see page 280)
1 loaf of crusty white bread, cut into
  thick slices allowing 2 slices per
  person
about 2 tablespoons mayonnaise
  (see page 77)

Increase the oven temperature up to 220°C (425°F/ Gas 7). To roast the chicken, first pat it dry to remove any excess moisture inside and out. Fill the cavity with a handful or two of your stuffing, enough to fill the bird, keeping the rest for later. Rub the skin with a little butter, then season well with salt and pepper. Place in a roasting tin. Roast for around 35 minutes, then drop the heat to 160°C (315°F/Gas 2–3) and cook for a further 30 minutes. When cooked, remove the chicken from the oven, turn the chicken upside down so it is sitting breast side down and allow to cool — this will help keep the breast meat juicy.

When the chicken has cooled, remove the skin from the breast and slice it thinly (discard the skin from the legs as it tends to be too fatty). Shred the chicken meat. Put the skin and shredded meat into a bowl along with your stuffing and roasted corn kernels. In the roasting tin there should be some fat and juice — carefully strain off the fat, then tip the rest of the juices onto the chicken mixture. Add just enough mayonnaise to bind together.

To assemble your sandwiches, start by tossing your rocket with the red wine dressing in a large bowl. Lay out the bread and spread some mayonnaise on each slice. On half of the bread place your chicken salad, then a mound of rocket, add a little seasoning and top each sandwich with the remaining bread slices.

Duck breast in green peppercorns with pea and artichoke salad

Serves 4–6

This is a clean and fresh duck dish, perfect for a hot day when you want something satisfying. You can adjust the amount of peppercorns to suit yourself — I like it with a peppery bite so if you have a sensitive palate reduce the amount of peppercorns. If you can't get fresh peppercorns you can use 25 g (1 oz) dried peppercorns instead.

For the poached duck
breast and dressing

4 good-sized duck breasts (about 120 g/4¼ oz), skin on

300 ml (10½ fl oz) gewürztraminer or medium-bodied white wine

300 ml (10½ fl oz) duck or chicken stock (see page 76)

70 g (2½ oz) fresh green peppercorns (or 25 g/1 oz dried peppercorns)

100 ml (3½ fl oz) extra virgin olive oil

To make the poached duck breast, seal the duck breasts in a hot frying pan, starting skin side down — all you want is a nice golden colour, then flip them over and quickly seal the flesh side.

Pour the gewürztraminer and stock into a saucepan that is wide enough to fit the duck breasts side by side. Add the peppercorns. Bring to a simmer, then gently add the duck breasts and poach for about 15 minutes — this should give you slightly pink flesh. When the duck is cooked to your liking, remove it from the poaching liquid and keep boiling the broth until it is reduced to a glaze — you should end up with about 150 ml (5 fl oz). Remove the pan from the heat and, while still warm, whisk in the oil. This is the dressing for the salad; set aside.

For the salad

100 g (3½ oz) peas in the pod

2 heads of celery

2 artichokes

a wedge of lemon

4 radishes

100 g (3½ oz) sugar snap peas,
coarsely chopped

100 g (3½ oz) pickled vegetables
(either bought ones or home-made
from page 234)

1 bunch of chervil, coarsely
chopped

To make the salad, pod your peas, then blanch them in salted water for about 3 minutes until they are tender and sweet. Rinse under cold running water to stop the cooking process and set aside.

Remove all of the dark green outside stems of the celery; don't throw these away as they are still great to eat but it is the celery heart that is better suited for this salad (celery hearts are the small pale green insides of the celery).

Take the artichokes and start removing the outer leaves, one at a time. Keep going until you reach the yellow, tender leaves. Place one artichoke on its side; you should be able to see where the leaves finish and the heart begins. Using a sharp, serrated knife cut off the leaves. Working carefully, use a sharp paring knife or small vegetable knife to trim away the dark green exterior of the artichoke. Cut the stem about 2 cm (¾ inches) down from the base of the heart. Using a spoon, scrape out all of the spiky 'choke' from the centre of the artichoke heart. Rinse under cold water and then rub the heart well with a piece of cut lemon to stop the artichoke from turning brown. Repeat with the other artichoke.

Wash your radishes well, but leave on some of the stem — these are useful to hold on to as you slice your radish.

Using a mandolin or a sharp knife, thinly slice the celery, raw artichoke hearts and radish, then place in a bowl with the peas, sugar snap peas, pickled vegetables, chervil and about two-thirds of your dressing. Gently toss together.

To serve, divide the salad among plates. Slice the duck thinly and layer the strips over the top of the salad, then drizzle with the remaining dressing.

Brined and roasted quails with agresto sauce

Serves 6

I can easily eat two quails at a sitting so use this as a guide when thinking about how many to cook. I find that when it comes to presenting this dish I simply put all of the quails in the middle of the table and have everyone dig in. It is a good idea to provide finger bowls and napkins because the best way to eat a quail is with your fingers.

For the brined quail

3.5 litres (121 fl oz/14 cups) water
1 bunch of thyme
2 bay leaves
freshly ground black pepper
280 g (10 oz/1¼ cups) salt
250 g (9 oz/heaped 1 cup) sugar
12 whole quails
about 200 g (7 oz) butter, at room temperature

For the agresto sauce

125 g (4½ oz/heaped ¾ cup) almonds
125 g (4½ oz/1¼ cups) walnuts
1 clove of garlic, chopped
1 bunch of flat-leaf (Italian) parsley, leaves finely chopped
½ bunch of basil, leaves finely chopped
80 ml (2½ fl oz/⅓ cup) extra virgin olive oil
80 ml (2½ fl oz/⅓ cup) verjuice
1 teaspoon salt
freshly ground black pepper

To make the brined quail, pour the water into a large saucepan and bring to the boil. Add your herbs and pepper, then stir in the salt and sugar. As soon as the sugar and salt have dissolved, turn off the heat and allow to cool completely in the fridge.

Take your quails and clean any offal out of the cavity. When the brine is cold, add the quails to the brine and use a plate or cooling rack to weigh down the quails to ensure that they are totally submerged, then refrigerate for 3–4 hours.

Preheat your oven to 230°C (450°F/Gas 8). When you are ready to cook the birds, remove them from the brine and rinse in plenty of cold water, then pat dry. Take some of the butter in your hands and rub it all over the quails, then place them into a roasting tin and cook in the oven for 30 minutes, or until they are nicely browned. Remove them from the oven and allow to rest upside down in the roasting tin for a further 10 minutes.

To make the agresto sauce, place the nuts and the garlic into a food processor and blend finely, then transfer to a bowl and add your chopped herbs, olive oil and verjuice and mix really well — you should have a pasty 'pesto type' sauce. Now add your seasoning.

Once the quails have rested, you have the choice to either leave them whole or cut them. To cut them, place them onto a chopping board and insert the tip of a knife all the way into the cavity and cut down through the bottom of the bird. Turn the quail, breast side down, and open them up slightly, then cut through the middle of the breast. Remove the legs from the breast.

Place the quail pieces into your bowl of sauce. Toss well to ensure that they are really well coated, then transfer to a platter. I like to serve the quail with the potatoes fried in red wine and coriander seeds (see page 230).

Salt-baked chicken

Serves 4–6

A salt dough has an advantage over a salt crust, which is that you effectively create a small portable oven around your food. This means that you can start the cooking process at home, then the heat inside the dough will finish the cooking while you're on the way to your picnic or friend's house. Both easy and impressive. Serve the chicken with the citrus and spice dressing on page 127.

For the salt dough
1 kg (2 lb 4 oz) plain (all-purpose) flour
1 kg (2 lb 4 oz) flossy salt
about 550 ml (19 fl oz) water or enough to make the dough malleable

For salt-baked chicken
1.8–2 kg (4–4 lb 8 oz) whole organic chicken
1 quantity dressing (see page 127), to serve

For the salt dough, use coarse flossy or kosher salt rather than table salt; table salt dissolves quickly and can make your meat taste salty. Fancy sea salts are better used elsewhere; for this process it is a waste.

To make the salt dough, combine the flour and salt in a large bowl. Make a well in the middle and add most of the water. Don't add all the water — it is easier to add more water to a dry dough than to add more flour to a wet dough. What you are looking for is a firm yet malleable dough. Start by kneading with your hands — this will take a bit of work. Once your dough is made, place it in a bowl and cover with plastic wrap; it will need to rest for 1 hour. If you refrigerate your dough, remove it from the fridge and allow it to come to room temperature as this will be easier to roll.

Roll out your dough on a well-floured bench until about 5 mm (¼ inch) thick; you may want to do this in two pieces for ease. Place the dough on a baking tray.

Preheat your oven to 190–200°C (375–400°F/Gas 5–6). To make the salt-baked chicken, arrange the wings of the chicken under the bird and gently pull the legs away from the body slightly; now pat dry inside and out. If you want to stuff the cavity, use the squeezed blood orange and lemon peels from the dressing and a small head of fennel with the fronds attached (it's fine if the fronds stick out a bit).

Put the chicken, breast side down, onto the middle of your dough and wrap it completely, making sure that it is totally covered. Roll the chicken over so it sits breast side up and cook in the oven for 50 minutes–1 hour. Rest for about 30–40 minutes before eating.

When you are ready to serve you will need to open the crust — do this by using the heel of a large heavy chopping knife and hack into the base of the dough, working all the way around; you will then be creating a 'dish with a lid'. Take this to the table and remove the lid. Serve with the dressing on the side.

Bacon and egg pie

Serves 4–6

10 g (¼ oz) butter
1 kg (2 lb 4 oz) button mushrooms,
  chopped
salt and freshly ground black pepper
4 ripe roma (plum) tomatoes
2 x 25 cm (10 inch) square sheets
  of bought puff pastry
20 thin slices bacon or speck
10 eggs
1 small handful flat-leaf (Italian)
  parsley, chopped

Heat the butter in a large heavy-based saucepan over medium–high heat. Add the mushroom, season with a little salt and pepper, and cook for about 20 minutes, stirring often, until the mushrooms form an aromatic paste. Remove from the heat and allow to cool.

Cut the tomatoes in half crossways and use a spoon to scoop out the seeds and soft centres (you can use these in a sauce or stock). Spoon the cool mushroom paste inside each tomato shell and set aside.

Preheat your oven to 220°C (425°F/Gas 7). Lightly grease a shallow rectangular baking tin. Line the tin with the puff pastry and gently press into the base and sides, trimming any excess pastry. Bake for about 18 minutes, or until golden. Remove from the oven and while the pastry is still hot, use a clean tea towel (dish cloth) to push the pastry down into the dish so that it is flat. Set aside to cool.

Reduce the oven temperature to 200°C (400°F/Gas 6). Scatter the bacon over the cooled pastry in the dish, then arrange the stuffed tomato halves over the top so that they are evenly spaced. Crack the eggs between the tomato — you will need to add enough eggs so that the pie is filled (the number of eggs will depend on the size of your egg and the size of your tomato). Bake the pie in the oven for about 20 minutes, or until set. Scatter with parsley, cut into slices and serve warm.

Duck and onion sandwich

Serves 6–8

Sure, this is a sandwich, but it's not just an ordinary sandwich. It may seem like a lot of effort to go to, but the results are superb and it makes a great meal. The duck is prepared a day in advance, which gives the duck time to absorb the flavours from the marinade.

For the duck

1 bunch of thyme
2 cloves of garlic
salt and freshly ground black pepper
4 duck leg quarters with the bone in
4 white onions, cut into large dice
a splash of stock (any type) or water

For the salad

3 French shallots
salt and freshly ground black pepper
2 tablespoons white wine vinegar
625–950 g (1 lb 6 oz–2 lb 2 oz/
    2–3 cups) rock salt
400 g (14 oz) baby onions,
    unpeeled
100 ml (3½ fl oz) extra virgin olive oil
a few sprigs of thyme
2 firm but ripe pears such as
    josephine, corella or red danjou
½ bunch of flat-leaf (Italian)
    parsley, coarsely chopped or
    1 punnet baby coriander
    (cilantro), trimmed

To make the duck, take half of the thyme and 1 of the garlic cloves, chopping them and combining with salt and pepper. Rub this mixture thoroughly over your duck. Cover this and refrigerate overnight.

Preheat your oven to 200°C (400°F/Gas 6). When you are ready to cook the duck, place the duck leg quarters in a roasting tin with the chopped onion, remaining thyme and garlic and stock. Place this into the oven and cook, covered with foil or a lid, for about 2 hours. Remove the foil and cook, uncovered, for a further 20–30 minutes. You will need to stir the mixture regularly to ensure that everything cooks evenly.

To make the salad dressing, peel and very finely slice the French shallots, then mix together with a good pinch of salt, pepper and vinegar. Let this sit until your onions are ready — this will give the shallot time to pickle slightly.

Preheat your oven to 200°C (400°F/Gas 6), pour a bed of salt onto your roasting tray and stand your onions, root side down, on the salt. This will keep the onions from making contact with the roasting tray and will keep them at an even dry heat. It will take about 25 minutes to cook the onions; to test them for doneness, push a sharp knife into them — they should be very soft all the way through. Leave the oven on.

When they are cool enough to handle, use a sharp knife to cut off the hard root of the onion and remove the skins; if cooked correctly the onions should just about fall out of the skins. Place all the onions in a bowl and drizzle with a little of the extra virgin olive oil and add a few sprigs of thyme and let this sit until you are ready to serve.

Cut the pears in half and remove the cores. Using a mandolin or a sharp knife, cut thin slivers of pear and add to the onions along with the parsley. Finish your dressing by whisking the remaining olive oil into the shallot mixture, then pour over your salad and gently fold to combine.

For serving

1 loaf of Turkish (flat) bread, focaccia or schiacciata

Once the duck is tender, remove from the oven but keep the oven on. When cool enough to handle, remove the duck legs and place onto a chopping board. Remove the skin and bone from the duck and place the meat into a large bowl. Using a wooden spoon, mash the meat up until it is well shredded so that there are no pieces of duck, just a smooth mixture of meat. Now add the onions from the duck and mash this mixture together really well, taste for seasoning and if all is good it is ready to stuff your bread with.

Split the bread open lengthways and open up (I find it easier to leave the loaf whole and cut into pieces afterwards). Now spread your duck and onion mix over the bread in a thick layer and close the bread up. The size you cut the sandwiches depends on how you want to serve them. Since I like to get everyone to share everything, I always prefer to cut them into about 4 cm (1½ inch) wide strips, which I then put back in the oven for about 10 minutes until hot in the middle and nice and crunchy on the outside. Arrange your sandwiches on a platter and serve the salad on the side.

Poached and crumbed duck wings

Serves 6

Use this recipe as a guide to quantities — either serve two duck wings per person for an appetiser or allow six wings per person for great beer food. The idea with this recipe is that when you are cooking duck, you remove the wings and pop them in the freezer. Once you have collected a few you can defrost them and prepare this crunchy treat.

12 duck wings
300 ml (10½ fl oz) sweet sherry
a dollop of dijon mustard
about 300 g (10½ oz/3¾ cups)
    fresh or 300 g (10½ oz/3 cups) dry
    breadcrumbs (see note page 297)
500 ml (17 fl oz /2 cups) vegetable
    or canola oil
salt
pickled cauliflower sauce (see
    page 234), to serve

When you look at your duck wings, you will see that they are made up of three segments joined by two joints. Cut through the joints to make into three pieces, then throw away the wing 'tip' as there is not really anything there worthwhile eating. Place the wing pieces in a saucepan that allows them to fit snugly, then cover with the sherry. Bring the sherry up to a very gentle simmer and cook for about 45 minutes. If you are using a gas stove be careful that the sherry doesn't catch on fire. If you do flambé the poaching liquor don't panic — as soon as the alcohol has burnt away the flames will die.

Remove the pan from the heat and allow the wing pieces to cool in the sherry. When they are cool enough to handle but not completely cold, lift the wings out of the liquid. The middle segments of wings have two bones: remove one of the bones by taking the nugget of skin in one hand and gently twisting out the bone with the other.

Once you have removed all of the wings, put the liquid back on the stove and reduce for 10–12 minutes over a high heat until you have a thick syrup, then set to one side. Take your wings and brush with a little of the mustard, then toss in the breadcrumbs. You are about to deep-fry — please be careful! A good safety tip is to only fill your pan by one-third — this will give the oil room to boil up without spilling over the side of the pan. Heat some vegetable oil in a large saucepan. One way to tell if the oil is hot enough is to place the handle of a wooden spoon into the oil; if little bubbles appear, your oil is ready. Deep-fry the duck pieces until golden — you may need to do this in batches. Using a slotted spoon remove them from the oil and drain on paper towels, then season with salt. Transfer to a plate.

To serve, drizzle a little of the reduced sherry over the duck wings and place next to a dollop of pickled cauliflower sauce. Serve immediately with a bottle of good ale.

Cockie-leekie

Serves 8

This dish is as Scottish as bagpipes, haggis and blokes in skirts. It is a great feel-good family dish that always lasts for at least two meals and the name makes kids laugh. I like to add a little pearl barley to mine which is not quite sticking with tradition but I find that it provides a little more body.

500 g (1 lb 2 oz/2¼ cups) pitted
  prunes
165 g (5¾ oz/¾ cup) pearl barley
1 kg (2 lb 4 oz) piece of brisket, cut
  in half
1.5 kg (3 lb 5 oz) leeks, white parts
  thinly sliced, the green bits tied
  together to flavour the stock
1 litre (35 fl oz/4 cups) chicken
  stock (see page 74)
2 litres (70 fl oz/8 cups) water
2 teaspoons salt
freshly ground black pepper
1.8 kg (4 lb) whole boiling chicken
  (see note page 78)

Cover the prunes with water and soak overnight. Cover the pearl barley in water and also soak overnight. The next day strain, then separately rinse both the prunes and barley and keep separate.

In a pot large enough to fit the chicken later (you'll need one of about 4.5 litres/157 fl oz/18-cup capacity), put in the beef, tied leek ends, stock and water. Season with the salt and pepper. Bring the heat up but try not to let it boil, you want a nice gentle simmer. Skim off the grey bubbles as they rise but leave any fat on the surface of the broth. Fat carries flavour, so skimming off the fat at the early stage of cooking means that you are throwing away perfectly good flavour. If you maintain a gentle simmer that does not allow the fat to boil back into your broth you will have a perfectly clear and well-flavoured broth; you can skim it off at the end if you like.

After about 1 hour of simmering add the soaked and rinsed barley — you will need to very gently stir the barley from time to time throughout cooking. Half an hour later, add the chicken. At this stage you may also need to add another litre (35 fl oz/4 cups) of water if it has evaporated too much. An hour later remove the leek ends, then add the prunes and cook for 10 minutes before adding the white part of the leeks and cooking for a final 10 minutes — ideally the leeks should retain a slight crunch to them.

The proper way to serve cockie-leekie is in a shallow bowl: place a piece each of beef and chicken and some leeks, barley and prunes in a bowl and pour on the broth. The lazy and fun way to serve it is by taking the pot to the table with a carving fork, sharp knife and a ladle and letting your guests eat way too much.

Sautéed duck livers and prosciutto on toast

Serves 4

This is a great lunch dish — the rich livers are cut with salty prosciutto and peppery rocket. Different breeds of duck and different suppliers will produce livers that vary in size. The ones I've used are about 50–60 g (1¾–2¼ oz) each.

For the dressing
100 g (3½ oz/1 cup) walnuts
1 tablespoon grated orange zest
juice of 1 orange
60 ml (2 fl oz/¼ cup) balsamic cider vinegar or balsamic vinegar
80 ml (2½ fl oz/⅓ cup) extra virgin olive oil
salt and freshly ground black pepper

For the sautéed livers and prosciutto
800 g (1 lb 12 oz) duck livers
1 sage leaf per liver
½ slice of prosciutto per liver
seasoned flour
3–4 tablespoons clarified duck fat (see page 75) or vegetable oil
4 large handfuls of rocket (arugula)
salt and freshly ground black pepper
4 thick slices of good sourdough toast

To make the dressing, toast the walnuts by putting them in a 150°C (300°F/Gas 2) oven for 5–7 minutes until they are just starting to colour. If they become too dark they will taste bitter and will ruin the dish. Rub them with a clean cloth to remove the skin. Put the walnuts in a mortar and pestle or food processor and grind or blend. As you are working the walnuts, slowly add the orange zest and juice and vinegar, then the olive oil. Add your seasoning.

To make the sautéed livers and prosciutto, clean the livers free of any tubes and bits, then place each one on a sage leaf. Wrap each liver snuggly in prosciutto, then secure with a toothpick. Lightly coat the prosciutto-wrapped livers in seasoned flour and fry in a hot frying pan with just a little duck fat or oil. Cook on a high heat until well coloured, about 3 minutes on one side, then 2 minutes on the other, this will give you nice pink livers — if you prefer them cooked more, turn one more time and give another couple of minutes.

Tip your livers onto a clean cloth to drain, then remove any excess fat from the pan. Add the rocket and a touch of seasoning to the pan and cook briefly, moving often to ensure even cooking. Place the rocket in a mound on each piece of toast. Add the dressing to your cooling pan as the heat of the pan will loosen the dressing and get the flavours going — return your livers to this and coat them well. Place the livers on your rocket and drizzle with any remaining dressing.

Duck confit

Serves 2–4

Duck confit is regarded as a French classic, but its origins go way back to the ancient Greeks and Romans. Today, chefs have science on their side and have worked out everything from the exact temperature of the fat to the pH level of the salted meat, but it really needn't be so complicated. Often restaurants only preserve the duck leg. I have put together this recipe because it is easy to do at home and uses one whole fatty duck so you have no bits left over.

1 fat duck, about 2.5 kg (5 lb 8 oz) (if you have an obliging butcher, ask to have the duck cut into four pieces)

250 ml (9 fl oz/1 cup) water

120 g (4¼ oz/1 scant cup) coarse sea salt

2 juniper berries, crushed

2 cloves, crushed

4 bay leaves

1 bunch of thyme, leaves only

2 cloves of garlic, crushed

vegetable oil (optional)

Collect all the fat you can from the cavity and any fat on the offal of the duck, then remove the skin from the whole duck including the neck — this will take a good bit of pulling and a little trimming with a sharp knife. Place the fat, skin and water in a heavy-based saucepan. Boil over a high heat and stir from time to time. After about 20 minutes you need to start watching the fat — it should be a milky, bubbly mass. As the water evaporates the fat will start to become clear and after 30–40 minutes the fat will become completely clear and golden. Remove from the heat and pass through a fine sieve. Refrigerate until needed.

If your duck is whole, cut it into four pieces. Start by removing the legs, leaving the thigh and drumstick together, then split the breast down the middle and chop away the bones on the leg side of the duck. Leave all of the meat on the bone. Mix the salt, spices, herbs and garlic together and sprinkle over the duck meat, cover with plastic wrap and leave to sit in the fridge overnight. The next day, rinse the duck in plenty of cold water — do this over a sieve so that you are able to catch the spices and put them back onto the duck. Put the duck along with its reserved coating of herbs and garlic in an ovenproof dish that is large enough to take the duck and duck fat but only come halfway up the side of the dish (a 3 litre/104 fl oz/12-cup dish will suffice).

Preheat your oven to 110°C (225°F/Gas ½). Melt your duck fat but don't let it get too hot. The temperature of the fat should be around 75–80°C (165–175°F). You can test this by very carefully touching the fat — it should feel hot but not burn you. Pour the fat over your duck, making sure that the meat is completely submerged (you can cheat by topping up

Allow one piece of duck per person. Confit is preserved meat, which means that there is danger of bacteria that can cause spoilage — don't worry as it is a very low risk if you make sure that all of your equipment and your hands are clean and dry and that your raw ingredients do not sit at room temperature any longer than necessary.

with vegetable oil if you don't quite have enough fat, but it is preferable to use pure duck fat). Once you have poured on the fat, cover it with a sheet of baking paper to ensure the duck is completely covered during the cooking process.

Put the duck in the oven. The confit is ready when a knife inserted into one of the legs reveals that the meat is tender all the way down to the bone — this will take about 2½–3 hours. Remove the duck and place it in a wide-mouthed 1.5 litre (52 fl oz/6-cup) sterilised ceramic pot, glass jar or container that you wish to store your confit in. Strain the fat into a clean saucepan, place on a high heat and boil until it has become clear again, then pour it over the duck until the duck is completely covered. Any extra fat can be kept in a sterilised jar in the fridge and used for cooking or for your next batch of confit. Allow to cool completely before covering. The duck meat, if covered correctly, will keep for at least 3–4 weeks in the fridge. Your confit is ready to serve straight away, but it is best if it is allowed to sit in the fridge for a few days. When you use the meat, keep the fat and re-use for the next batch of confit or to roast potatoes.

Duck confit is best eaten warm. To reheat it you can simply pull the duck out of the fat and place in a hot oven or under a hot grill (broiler) for a few minutes. Duck confit has a hearty flavour that goes well with braised cabbage, red wine, mustards and pickles.

Duck rillettes

Serves 8–10

Rillettes (pronounced ree-yeht) is best thought of as a coarse meat pâté. It is the big boy of duck dishes as it is extremely rich and is best enjoyed in small quantities on warm toast alongside some pickles or cornichons. I like to make it from the confit leg instead of the breast meat, which tends to make the rillettes pasty. Temperature is the trick with this recipe — you want the fat and the meat to be coolish, but not so cool as to start to set when you start working the rillettes.

200 g (7 oz) duck confit meat (page
   100), removed from the leg at
   room temperature
salt and freshly ground black pepper
150 ml (5 fl oz) clarified duck fat
   (see page 75), at room
   temperature

To make rillettes, you start by making confit (see page 100) so you are effectively making two different dishes at the same time. By that I mean that if you preserve a whole duck you can store the breast meat for later use, then use the legs to make your rillettes. If you end up with slightly more or less meat than this recipe calls for, just adjust the fat and seasoning accordingly.

Put the duck meat in a large, clean, dry bowl and, using a clean, dry, stiff spatula, start to mash the duck meat until completely shredded. You may need to single out some stubborn pieces and give them a bit of extra work. A sign of a well-made rillettes is that there are no pieces of duck, just a smooth pâté of meat. You need to keep mixing your meat for the duration of this process, which can take 30 minutes to an hour — you'll get a sore arm, but just think of it as burning off the calories before ingesting them!

When you are happy with the consistency of the meat, add your seasoning, then start to pour in the fat a dash at a time, you will need to mix in around 100 ml (3½ fl oz) or half fat to the amount of meat. When everything is well combined check the seasoning again; I prefer mine to have lots of salt and to be quite peppery, but that's up to you.

When you're completely happy put the rillettes into a very clean, dry 300 ml (10½ fl oz) ramekin, pot or jar and refrigerate to allow to set. Leave the remainder of the clarified duck fat at room temperature, then place in a large bowl and use a whisk to whip until creamy and white. Use a spatula and place a layer of the fat over your rillettes — this layer of fat can be scraped off before serving; its job is to preserve your rillettes. If unopened this will keep perfectly well in the refrigerator for at least 2–3 weeks even though it usually gets eaten well before then.

Butcher

Bacon hash

Serves 4

In 1997 I went to Los Angeles and stumbled upon a place called the Pot Sticker Café. The place was one big breakfast joint and offered all the coffee you could drink. Every now and then I enjoy a meal so much that all I want to do is recapture the experience of eating it. The hash I was served here was freshly fried and full of flavour. Use this recipe wisely as its powers should only be used for good; it is ideal for 'the morning after'.

300 g (10½ oz) piece of speck, diced into 1 cm (½ inch) cubes (you'll need to go to a butcher or delicatessen for this)
500 g (1 lb 2 oz) onions, diced into 1 cm (½ inch) cubes
2 cloves of garlic, finely chopped
a few stalks of rosemary
600 g (1 lb 5 oz) all-purpose potatoes (such as desiree), diced into 1 cm (½ inch) cubes (don't peel the potatoes)
a dash of oil

Preheat your oven to 180°C (350°F/Gas 4). Put the speck in a large casserole dish and place in the oven. Stir the speck from time to time to ensure even cooking. As the speck cooks it will release most of its fat — resist the urge to tip this off as it is all needed. When the speck is just starting to give when you press it with a spoon and it has become golden brown, about 30 minutes, add the onion, garlic and rosemary, stir well, then put back in the oven. You want the onion to cook right down and start to colour; you will need to stir a couple of times during this stage as it will take another 30 minutes.

Now add the diced potato and fold it through the bacon and onion, then return to the oven. You want to keep cooking until your potato is tender, about another 30 minutes. Remove the rosemary stalks. If you are really impatient this can be eaten straight away, but the best way to serve this is to allow it to cool completely then place into a hot frying pan with a little oil and fry up till nice and golden. I like this served with poached eggs (see page 75), toast and juicy, ripe tomatoes.

Bresaola with peas and marjoram

Serves 8

Bresaola is an air-dried beef that is usually made from silverside. The raw meat is cured in a mixture of red wine, herbs (such as rosemary and bay leaves) and spices (such as pepper and cloves). After it has been preserved in the brine it is then allowed to air dry, which gives the beef its distinct flavour and texture. You can buy bresaola from Italian delicatessens; you should always make sure that it is being sliced as you order. This will not only ensure that it is soft and full of flavour, but also that it is being sliced as thinly as possible. Bresaola works really well with the sweetness of the peas and marjoram in this dish, but you can substitute the bresaola for prosciutto if you prefer.

300 g (10½ oz) fresh green peas, podded
a few sprigs of marjoram
salt and freshly ground black pepper
125 ml (4 fl oz/½ cup) extra virgin olive oil
about 16 thin slices of bresaola
a small piece of parmesan cheese, grated

Take your peas and blanch them in salted water for about 2–3 minutes, then drain and immerse straight away into iced water to stop the cooking process. Drain again.

Place the peas into a large mortar, remove the leaves of the marjoram and add to the peas, then crush everything together with some salt, pepper and about half of the olive oil. You don't want a purée — just crush until you have a coarse mash.

Arrange your bresaola on a plate, then drizzle with the remaining olive oil and season with a little salt and pepper. Place a mound of the peas on your beef, then finish with some freshly grated parmesan cheese.

Toasted reuben sandwich

Serves 4

This sandwich is named after its creator Arthur Reuben, owner of Reuben's Delicatessen, which no longer exists, but in its day was one of New York's more famous delicatessens. When you buy one of these in New York, you usually receive about 2 kg (4 lb 8 oz) of pastrami, a foot-deep pile of sauerkraut stuck together by a mountain of melted Swiss cheese wedged between two bits of rye bread and, just to make it subtle, a foot-long pickle on the side of the plate. I find most people in Sydney are a little concerned about eating that much protein and vinegar in one sitting, so this sandwich is a bit more modest.

1 loaf of fresh ciabatta or other
  crusty white bread
some dijon mustard to scrape on
  the bread
16 slices of cooked corned beef
  (see page 116)
8 slices of tilsit, gruyère, fontina or
  Swiss cheese
100 g (3½ oz) drained sauerkraut
salt and freshly ground black pepper
pickled vegetables (either bought
  ones or home-made from page
  234)
a dollop of wholegrain mustard

You can buy pre-cooked corned beef for this sandwich but I would recommend cooking yourself a piece for dinner one night (see page 116) and making sandwiches with the leftovers. Sauerkraut is available from most large supermarkets and delicatessens.

I like to cut the bread on an angle, which will give you a large, round slice of bread on which to build your sandwich — you'll need eight slices of bread. On each slice add a thin scraping of dijon mustard, two slices of meat, one slice of cheese and some of the sauerkraut. Season with salt and pepper and close your sandwiches up. What you end up with is the sauerkraut in the middle surrounded by cheese, then by corned beef and bread.

To cook your sandwiches either use a sandwich press or, if you don't have one, cook them in a large frying pan that's placed over a medium heat — I don't worry about any oil or butter as they should not stick. If you are using a frying pan, keep squashing the sandwiches down; when golden brown, turn over and repeat on the other side. What you are looking for is a crispy, golden sandwich that is hot all the way through. The best way to tell it is ready is to press the sandwich with your fingers — if the cheese oozes from the sides it is done.

Cut in half and serve alongside some of your pickled vegetables and a dollop of wholegrain mustard.

Glazed leg of ham

Serves 12–14

In my neck of the woods Christmas is smack bang in the middle of summer and for me Christmas isn't Christmas without a leg of ham. In my family it is considered a complete failure of the festive season if there is not still some leftover ham, hidden under a tea towel, until at least January 14th. In fact, by then you must have had fried ham and eggs at least twice, eaten half a dozen ham and cheddar sandwiches, made a couple of ham pizzas, come home late and chewed on the bone while drunk and still have Mum in the background saying 'I wish you lot would finish this ham so I can make soup!'.

8 or 9 kg (18 lb or 20 lb 4 oz) leg of ham, bone in
2 teaspoons black peppercorns
2 juniper berries
4 cloves
1 allspice berry
2 cm (¾ inch) piece of cinnamon
300 g (10½ oz/1⅓ cups) demerara sugar
100 g (3½ oz/heaped ⅓ cup) dijon mustard
300 ml (10½ fl oz) apple juice

Take your ham and gently peel away the skin, making sure that you leave all the fat where it is. I will slap your hand if I catch you removing the fat before it is cooked — it has a job to do during the cooking process; you can take it off (if you must) after the ham has cooked and cooled.

Preheat your oven to 180°C (350°F/Gas 4). Gently toast your spices in a dry frying pan, then pound them together in your mortar and pestle. Mix this with the sugar. Now it is time to get messy: use your hands to rub the entire ham in dijon mustard. Wash and dry your hands. Sit the ham on a wire rack in a roasting tin, then pat on your spiced sugar — some of it will fall off into the pan, which is fine. Pour in some water to keep the bottom of the pan from burning. Bake for about 20 minutes, then remove and baste with a little of the apple juice; repeat this process every 10 minutes, basting with the apple juice and pan juices, for about 1 hour or until you have a beautiful, fragrant ham with a lovely golden glaze. Allow to cool completely. You can keep the basting glaze as a sauce to serve with the ham.

To store your ham, do not cover with plastic wrap as this will cause your ham to sweat; instead use a tea towel (dish cloth), or even better, a pillowcase with 'Merry Christmas' or a picture of a smiling Santa on it. I like to serve my ham simply with just a potato salad and pickled and spiced cherries (see page 248).

Beef cheek burgers with cabbage and beetroot

Serves 6

For the beef cheek patties

1 kg (2 lb 4 oz) beef cheeks,
  trimmed of excess fat
a little seasoned plain (all-purpose)
  flour
duck fat or oil, for frying
1 kg (2 lb 4 oz) onions, diced
2 cloves of garlic, diced
a few sprigs of thyme
salt and freshly ground black pepper
600 ml (21 fl oz) red wine
2 tablespoons hot mustard
a few sprigs of flat-leaf (Italian)
  parsley, leaves chopped
400 g (14 oz) fresh pork caul

For the beetroot

about 1 kg (2 lb 4 oz) table salt
4 large beetroots (beets), skins on
  and leaves removed
salt and freshly ground black pepper
a splash of truffle oil
a splash of olive oil

 Caul is a fine membrane from the stomach of a pig, and has a wonderful ability to hold the beef filling during the cooking process but, by the end of cooking, it will almost have completely dissolved. You may need to plan ahead and order it in advance from your butcher.

Preheat your oven to 180°C (350°F/Gas 4). To make the patties, start by placing a large flameproof casserole dish over high heat. Lightly coat the beef cheeks in a little flour and fry them in the duck fat or oil until they are a good brown colour. Remove the beef from the dish and tip off any burnt or excess oil — do not wipe your dish but instead add a little more fresh fat or oil. Return the dish to the heat and cook the onion with the garlic, thyme, salt and pepper until the onion is soft, then return the beef to the dish and add the wine — the cheeks need to be completely covered, so you may need to add a little water. Bring to the boil on your stove, then cover with a tight-fitting lid and transfer to the oven for at least 2 hours, or until the they are completely soft. During the cooking process you will need to turn the cheeks from time to time to ensure even cooking. Remove them from the liquid and reserve the liquid in a container. When cool enough to handle, shred the meat and place into a large bowl, then add the mustard, parsley and seasoning and stir to coat.

Rinse the caul in plenty of cold water. Take hold of a piece and unravel a nice large sheet of the caul and place onto your chopping board. Using one-sixth of the beef mixture, roll into a ball and press to create a patty shape before placing onto the caul. Take up the edges of the caul to wrap the filling completely, trimming away any excess caul. Repeat with the remaining caul and beef to make six patties. Refrigerate until ready to cook.

To make the beetroot, make a bed of salt on a baking tray and nestle in the beetroots. Bake for about 25 minutes, or until the beetroots are tender when tested with a knife. Remove from the salt and set to one side until they are cool enough to handle but before they get completely cold. Wearing gloves, scrape away the skin and thinly slice the beetroot and then place into a small bowl, season with salt and pepper and add a little truffle oil and olive oil. The beetroots are best if they are done a couple of hours in advance and then left out at room temperature.

For the buttered cabbage

½ small savoy cabbage
a knob of butter
salt and freshly ground black pepper

For serving

1 loaf of unsliced sandwich bread or
   6 burger buns
softened butter
vegetable oil

To make the buttered cabbage, shred the cabbage as finely as you can with a sharp knife and set aside until you are ready to start cooking. You only want to cook the cabbage for the briefest moment so leave it until you are just about ready to serve. In a saucepan, add the butter and a splash of water and place over high heat. When the butter has melted, add the cabbage and the seasoning and mix the cabbage with a spoon until it has softened and is well coated with the butter. Place the cabbage into a colander to strain off any excess liquid.

Preheat your oven to 160°C (315°F/Gas 2–3). Cut 12 slices from the bread loaf, if using, then cut rings from each slice using a round cutter that is roughly the same size or bigger than your patties. Brush each side of the bread with softened butter (or butter the inside of the buns) and bake for about 8 minutes, or until golden and toasted.

In a large ovenproof frying pan, heat a little oil and cook the patties until brown on one side, then flip over and cook for another couple of minutes. Add all of the reserved sauce from the beef cheeks, then place the pan into the oven for 10–12 minutes, or until the patties are golden and the sauce they are sitting in is well reduced and rich. Place a slice of bread on each serving plate, then some drained cabbage, beetroot and finish with one of the patties and a good drizzle of the sauce before topping with the remaining bread slices. I like to serve these with fries (see pages 212–213).

Corned beef with buttered vegetables

Serves 6

This is the ultimate nana food! The recipe is written using 2 kg (4 lb 8 oz) of beef, which will feed six people and leave enough for a couple of toasted reuben sandwiches (see page 110). It makes wonderful dinner served with buttered vegetables and the parsley sauce recipe on page 233.

For the spice paste
1 tablespoon juniper berries
1 tablespoon black peppercorns
1 clove of garlic, chopped

For the corned beef
2 kg (4 lb 8 oz) uncooked corned
  silverside
400 ml (14 fl oz) balsamic vinegar
100 g (3½ oz/heaped ⅓ cup)
  tomato base (see page 228) or
  tomato paste (concentrated purée)
300 g (10½ oz/heaped 1⅔ cups)
  soft brown sugar
6 bay leaves
200 ml (7 fl oz) chicken stock (see
  page 79)
500 ml (17 fl oz) water

For the buttered vegetables
12 baby carrots, peeled
8 baby turnips, peeled
8 small new potatoes
1 tablespoon salt
a knob of butter
1 tablespoon wholegrain mustard
a generous pinch of chopped
  flat-leaf (Italian) parsley
salt and freshly ground black pepper

To make the spice paste, grind the juniper berries and pepper with a mortar and pestle, then add the garlic and pound into a paste. Rub your spice paste on to the corned silverside, cover with plastic wrap and let it sit overnight in the fridge.

Preheat your oven to 200°C (400°F/Gas 6). Put the corned beef in a large cast-iron pan or a casserole dish, fat side down, with the vinegar, tomato base, sugar, bay leaves, stock and water. Cover the pot with a lid and cook in the oven for about 1½ hours. Check from time to time to make sure that it doesn't dry out, adding water as needed. While you're in there give your beef a baste with the cooking liquid. After about 1½ hours take the lid off the pan and turn the beef so the fat side is facing up and cook for another hour — it is very important to continue basting the beef every 15 minutes or so.

Meanwhile, make the buttered vegetables. Boil the vegetables in well-salted water. The carrots and turnips can be cooked together if they are of similar size (8–12 minutes in boiling water), but I recommend cooking the potatoes separately (about 20 minutes starting with cold water). Place all of the hot vegetables in a bowl and gently toss in the butter, mustard, parsley and season with a little salt and pepper — you may need to splash in a little hot water to help things along.

When the beef is cooked, cut it into slices and serve with buttered vegetables and the parsley sauce (see page 233).

Roasted scotch fillet with watercress and beetroot salad

Serves 6

Scotch fillet is a great roasting meat, but only if it is of exceptional quality and has been allowed to hang, otherwise it can be a little tough. If you are roasting it don't serve it too rare, you want the heat to penetrate right through the meat. Cook until about medium–rare and allow to rest for a long time (at least half of your cooking time). This recipe suits a hot day when you need to feed a lot of people but don't have much time on your hands.

For the scotch fillet
salt and freshly ground black pepper
1 kg (2 lb 4 oz) whole piece of
   scotch fillet
1 large onion, thinly sliced
2 cloves of garlic, thinly sliced
1 stalk of rosemary, leaves only

Preheat your oven to 240°C (475°F/Gas 8). Start by seasoning the beef well, then seal it all over in a hot frying pan until really well coloured. Remove the meat from the pan and put it in a large bowl. Add the onion, garlic and rosemary to the bowl and squash and roll the onion onto the meat. Now place the beef along with the onion in a roasting tin and put it in the oven for 20 minutes. Turn the oven down to 220°C (425°F/Gas 7) and cook for a further 25–30 minutes for medium–rare. The trick is to keep turning your meat every few minutes to ensure even cooking and to caramelize the onion onto the outside of your beef.

When cooked to how you like (I recommend medium–rare to medium–well done) take out of the oven and allow to rest, reserving any cooking juices and the onion to make the dressing. Now, because of the nature of this dish, the beef does not need to be piping hot so this will give you plenty of time to make the salad and the dressing.

As a rule of thumb, for every 1 kg (2 lb 4 oz) of meat, cook in a preheated oven at 240°C (475°F/Gas 8) for 20 minutes, then turn the oven down to 220°C (425°F/Gas 7) and cook for 15–20 minutes for rare; 25–30 minutes for medium–rare; 35–45 minutes for medium; or 50–60 minutes for medium–well-done. Remember to allow your meat to rest for anywhere up to half of the total cooking time. You can always cook rare meat for longer but you can't cook overcooked meat less! And, if you are cooking for a group, offer well done cuts from the outside and rarer cuts from the middle.

For the dressing
100 ml (3½ fl oz) red wine vinegar
1 tablespoon wholegrain mustard
150 ml (5 fl oz) extra virgin olive oil
salt and freshly ground black pepper

For the salad
6 kipfler (fingerling) potatoes
6 baby beetroot (beets) with their
  leaves
1 bunch of watercress, picked from
  the stem
1 avocado, chopped
a few dried tomatoes (see note)

You can make the dried tomatoes yourself. Simply cut some roma (plum) tomatoes in half, place on a rack in your oven with just the pilot light on (or into a very low oven) overnight. You may need to repeat the following night if they are not dry enough.

To make the dressing, pour off the roasting juices from the roasting tin into a small saucepan (keep the onion to one side to add to the salad). Place over low heat and allow to reduce to almost a glaze. Remove from the heat and whisk in the vinegar, mustard and oil. Season with salt and pepper and set aside.

To make the salad, boil the potatoes in a saucepan of salted water for 5–10 minutes, or until tender — the time needed will depend on the size of your potatoes. Drain, then slice into 5 mm (¼ in) thick slices.

If you're worried about staining your hands when working with beetroot, it's a good idea to wear gloves. Remove the stems from the beetroots, keeping the leaves aside. Scrub the beetroots well. Pour most of the dressing into a large bowl. Using a mandolin or a sharp knife thinly slice the beetroots and add to the dressing, then add the beetroot leaves and allow to sit for a moment. Add the watercress, sliced potato, pieces of avocado, dry tomatoes and the onion that was roasted on the beef and gently fold the salad to mix the dressing and ingredients evenly.

To serve, thinly and neatly slice the meat. Serve by putting down a couple of thin slices of beef on a plate, then make a stack with alternating layers of salad and beef — you can either have two or three layers. To finish, drizzle with the remainder of the dressing.

Lamb shoulder and cardamom curry

Serves 4

If you don't know what some of these ingredients are, it's about time to venture to your local Indian spice shop. Take this recipe with you and point out what you want; while you are there, buy a couple of other things that you have never seen before. Don't forget to ask lots of questions; these little adventures are a great way to pick up secrets.

For the curry base

5 green cardamom pods

2 black cardamom pods (these look similar to green cardamom pods and have a sweeter and 'meatier' flavour)

1 teaspoon onion seeds or nigella seeds

1 teaspoon fenugreek seeds

½ teaspoon fennel seeds

½ teaspoon cumin seeds

150 g (5½ oz/1 scant cup) ghee

2 onions, finely diced

1 cm (½ inch) piece of fresh ginger, grated

2 cm (¾ inch) piece of fresh turmeric, grated

2 cloves of garlic, grated

3 large red chillies, chopped with the seeds left in

2 bay leaves

½ teaspoon ground asafoetida (be careful with this spice, a little goes a long way — too much will ruin your curry)

1 tablespoon salt

60 g (2¼ oz) palm sugar (jaggery), grated

500 ml (17 fl oz/2 cups) malt vinegar

To make the curry base, use a mortar and pestle to roughly grind together the cardamom (both types) and the onion, fenugreek, fennel and cumin seeds.

Melt the ghee in a heavy-based saucepan over high heat, then add the ground spices. Cook until they are golden or popping. Add the onion, ginger, turmeric, garlic, chilli, bay leaves, asafoetida and salt to the pan and cook until the onion is a rich brown colour, about 5 minutes, stirring often as it will stick easily.

Reduce the heat, add the palm sugar and vinegar and let everything cook down until you have a rich curry base; it will take about 20 minutes. Taste for seasoning; you want a powerful, hot curry base that is well balanced in flavour. Taste for salt (do you need to add more salt?), sour (add more vinegar?), sweet (add more palm sugar?), heat (add more chilli?). Allow to cool.

For the lamb
1.3 kg (3 lb) lamb shoulder, bone in
  (leave the fat on)
500 ml (17 fl oz/2 cups) chicken
  stock (see page 74)

For the tahini dressing
2½ tablespoons tahini
30 ml (1 fl oz) lemon juice
45 ml (1½ fl oz) water
salt and freshly ground black pepper
sugar (optional)

For serving
250 g (9 oz/5 cups) baby English
  spinach leaves
confit tomato (see page 229)
  (optional)
tempuring (see page 236) (optional)

You will need to make the curry base at least 1 day in advance so you can marinate the lamb in it overnight. The base will keep for 2 weeks, stored in an airtight container in the fridge.

To prepare the lamb, first rub it all over with all of the curry base, cover and marinate in the fridge overnight.

Preheat your oven to 170°C (325°F/Gas 3). Place the lamb and all of the curry base in a roasting tin and cover to halfway up the shoulder with chicken stock, then put in the oven. The lamb will take about 3 hours to cook, but throughout the cooking process you need to keep topping up the liquid if it reduces too much; also, you'll need to keep turning the lamb — as one side darkens expose the other. If you get to the point where your lamb is well coloured all over, the sauce is rich but the lamb still needs a little more cooking, just cover it with foil for the remainder of the cooking time. As a guide, cook uncovered for 2 hours and covered for 1 hour or when it starts to get dark. The lamb is cooked when the flesh falls off the bone.

To make the tahini dressing, put the tahini in a bowl, then whisk in the lemon juice, water, salt and pepper. As soon as you start to incorporate liquid it will thicken — adjust the consistency with water until it resembles pouring cream; I really like the slightly bitter flavour it has, but if you prefer you can add a little sugar.

To serve, scatter some baby spinach leaves over a platter, rip off the meat and place on top of the spinach, then pour on the curry sauce. I then like to squash some confit tomato over the top, letting all the tomato juice incorporate with the curry. Now, drizzle with some tahini dressing and serve alongside a big bowl of basmati rice and sprinkle with tempuring, if using.

Pot-roasted rabbit with tomato

Serves 4

Buying rabbit takes a bit of care. It is becoming more popular as more people are enjoying this wonderful sweet, lean meat. However, like any farmed product, there are those who deserve your support because they are producing a wonderful product in the right conditions and those you should avoid.

1.3 kg (3 lb) whole white rabbit
salt and freshly ground black pepper
a dash of oil
1 bunch of baby carrots, peeled, stalks removed
4 baby onions, cut in half
50 g (1¾ oz) piece of pancetta, cut into lardons
4 cloves of garlic, peeled but left whole
200 ml (7 fl oz) verjuice or sweet white wine and a dash of cider vinegar
500 ml (17 fl oz/2 cups) chicken stock (see page 74)
a few sprigs of thyme
250 g (9 oz) cherry tomatoes, cut in half
100 g (3½ oz) good-quality butter, chilled and chopped
1 handful of flat-leaf (Italian) parsley, chopped

Preheat your oven to 180°C (350°F/Gas 4). Cut your rabbit (or ask your butcher to do it for you) into the following pieces: remove and divide the legs, remove each of the shoulders, cut off the belly flap and cut into strips, chop the saddle and neck into four. Season with salt and pepper.

In a flameproof 4.5 litre (157 fl oz/18-cup) casserole dish add some oil and heat on top of your stove over a medium heat, then add the seasoned rabbit pieces, carrots, onions, pancetta and garlic and cook for about 10 minutes. When everything is a nice colour, deglaze the casserole with the verjuice (which basically means pour in your verjuice so that it lifts off the colour and flavour from the bottom of the casserole dish), then add the chicken stock and thyme, season and cover with a lid or foil, and cook in the oven for 35 minutes. Halfway through the cooking stir everything.

Poke your rabbit legs with a sharp knife, the meat should be tender to the bone and the juice run clear. Take the rabbit, vegetables and garlic and place them on a serving platter. Pour all of the remaining juice into a saucepan, add the tomatoes and bring to the boil. When the sauce has reduced slightly, start to whisk in small pieces of the cold butter. When it is all incorporated and looking foamy, remove from the heat, throw in the parsley and pour all of the sauce over the rabbit — it should sit in a little puddle of sauce. Serve in a deep bowl with lots of the sauce, a knife, fork and a spoon and a wedge of bread. I like to serve this dish alongside a fresh bean salad.

Salt-baked leg of lamb

Serves 6–8

There aren't many things tastier than salt-baked meats, but I wouldn't cook anything under 600 g (1 lb 5 oz) in a salt dough as you want the crust to have time to cook but you don't want to overcook your meat. Also, if you cook a small portion of meat in a salt dough it will become so salty as to be inedible. Make sure you cover the meat completely and check that the crust is intact. When you cook, the crust should go nice and brown and bake as hard as clay. Do not eat the crust — you may have to try it at least once because it looks lovely, but you will want a spitoon on hand and plenty of drinking water

1 tunnel-boned leg of lamb, shank left on (ask your butcher to do it for you), about 1.4 kg (3 lb 2 oz) boned weight
1 quantity of salt dough (see page 88)

Citrus and spice dressing
2 tablespoons fennel seeds, toasted
1 clove of garlic, peeled
3 tablespoons sugar
1 tablespoon salt
juice of 1 blood orange
juice of 2 lemons
a good dash of extra virgin olive oil

Preheat your oven to 200°C (400°F/Gas 6). If you'd like to, you can fill the cavity left by the bone with herbs such as rosemary, thyme and garlic. Cover the lamb in the salt dough so there are no gaps.

Cook the lamb in the oven for 55 minutes, then remove from the oven and let it rest for 45 minutes before eating.

To make the dressing, grind the fennel seeds with a mortar and pestle, then add the garlic, sugar and salt and crush into a paste. Add the juice from the orange and lemons and the oil. Taste for seasoning — you want a good balance of salty/sweet/sour.

When you are ready to serve you will need to open the crust — do this by using the heel of a large heavy chopping knife and hack into the base of the dough, working all the way around; you will then be creating a 'dish with a lid'. Take this to the table and remove the lid. Serve with the dressing on the side.

Roasted forerib with fresh horseradish sauce

Serves 4

The forerib is great roasted on the bone and it has nice layers of fat that keep the meat moist during cooking. Also, it is not too large, so a whole piece is not intimidating. Because of the nature of this cut, you can easily take one 'chop' and roast it for two people so use this as a rough guide as to how much to buy from your butcher (or allow 375 g/13 oz with bone per person). You may need to give a little advance warning when buying this cut on the bone so why not plan to get the butcher to hang the meat for a few days before you pick it up — the results are unquestionably better. Make sure that the fat is left on the meat and that the rib is not cut too short; you need to leave about 1–2 cm (½–¾ inches) bone from the eye of meat.

For the roasted forerib

1.5 kg (3 lb 5 oz) forerib, on the bone
salt and freshly ground black pepper
2 carrots, peeled and cut into quarters
1 onion, cut into quarters

Start by taking the forerib out of the fridge a couple of hours beforehand so it comes to room temperature.

Preheat your oven to 240°C (475°F/Gas 8). When you are ready to cook, season the meat all over with plenty of salt and pepper, then seal in a large roasting tin or frying pan until you have good colour all over. Place in a large roasting tin, fat side up and bone side down, either on a rack or on the carrot and onion — this will keep the meat off the bottom of the pan and ensure even cooking. Cook for 20 minutes, then turn the heat down to 220°C (425°F/Gas 7) and cook for a further 25–30 minutes for a medium–rare piece of beef. Now, rest your beef somewhere warm for up to half the total cooking time. You can keep the carrot and onion to serve with the roast, but they are mainly there to add flavour to the meat.

For the fresh horseradish sauce

200 ml (7 fl oz) extra virgin olive oil

100 g (3½ oz/1¼ cups) dry
  sourdough breadcrumbs (see
  page 297)

1 clove of garlic, finely chopped

300 g (10½ oz) piece of fresh
  horseradish, peeled and finely
  grated

60 ml (2 fl oz/¼ cup) red wine
  vinegar

salt and freshly ground black pepper

To make the horseradish sauce, heat some of the oil in a frying pan over low heat. Gently toast the breadcrumbs and garlic until golden and crispy. Allow to cool before using a mortar and pestle to pound into a paste with the horseradish and vinegar. Once you have a paste, carefully work in the remainder of the oil. Taste and adjust the consistency and seasoning to your liking — it will look a little like pesto.

To serve the meat, I like to remove the meat from the bone in the roasting tin — this way you will capture all of the wonderful roasting juices. Start removing the beef from the bones by sliding the knife just under the meat and on top of the ribs. Now slice off a portion by cutting across the meat and when you get to the bottom bone twist your knife sideways to remove the perfectly cooked, well-rested slab of beef. Place your beef on a warm plate, top with a dollop of horseradish sauce and spoon on some of the pan juices. I like to serve this simply with boiled potatoes and an iceberg lettuce salad.

As a rule of thumb the best way to cook forerib is to follow the guide on page 128. Another way to judge when the meat is done is the way I was taught when I first learnt to cook meat: I was shown how to 'feel' for doneness. Experience is the only way to guarantee precision on this one. However, I can share a little trick to help you understand this. Look at the palm of your hand relaxed with fingers out. Take the index finger of your other hand and gently push the fleshy part of your palm at the base of the thumb; this is how a rare steak should feel. Now, gently bring the index finger and thumb of your first hand together and touch that fleshy thumb part again; this is how meduim–rare feels. Thumb and middle finger is medium. Thumb and ring finger is medium–well done. Thumb and pinky is well done.

Braised lamb necks

Serves 4

I love eating lamb necks. I firmly believe that when you eat them you must gnaw at the bones to get the best out of them — they are full of flavour. I allow around one lamb's neck for two people. Ask if your butcher can clean the sinew off the back of them and cut them into pieces for you.

2 lamb necks, cleaned of excess fat and sinew, each cut into four pieces

seasoned flour, for dusting

about 150 ml (5 fl oz) vegetable oil

4 cloves of garlic, peeled but left whole

2 carrots, peeled and cut in half lengthways

1 large leek, cut into four short pieces

1 stalk of celery, cut into four short pieces

1 onion, quartered

a good splash of red wine

1 kg (2 lb 4 oz) tomatoes, chopped

60 g (2¼ oz/⅓ cup) pitted and chopped kalamata olives

1 tablespoon salted capers, rinsed and chopped

a few sprigs of thyme

2 bay leaves

1 teaspoon ground coriander seeds

salt and freshly ground black pepper

1 litre (35 fl oz/4 cups) chicken stock (see page 74) or beef stock

a handful of flat-leaf (Italian) parsley, chopped

Preheat your oven to 170°C (325°F/Gas 3). Coat the lamb necks in seasoned flour. Heat a frying pan until almost smoking hot to start, then turn down just slightly before adding the meat. Fry the lamb necks in oil until well coloured, then turn and colour the other side; you may need to do this in batches. Transfer the browned pieces of meat to a large casserole dish or roasting tin (you'll need one that is about 5 litres/175 fl oz/20-cup capacity). Tip off any burnt oil from the pan, add a dash of fresh oil and fry the garlic and vegetables (except the tomatoes) until they too are a golden brown, then add to the meat.

While the pan is still hot, deglaze it with the red wine: tip out the oil, then pour in enough red wine to cover the base of the pan and bring to a boil while using a wooden spoon to scrape up the browned goodness that has become stuck to the bottom of the pan. Pour this over the necks and vegetables, then add the tomatoes, olives, capers, thyme, bay leaves, coriander, salt and pepper and enough stock to almost cover the necks (a few pieces sticking out is okay). Place in the hot oven and braise, uncovered, for about 2½ hours. During the cooking process you will need to turn the meat over from time to time.

Towards the end of the cooking time, start to check your meat. You will know it is ready when the meat flakes away from the bone as you press it, also the sauce should be nice and shiny and have thickened. If you see that the meat is cooked but the sauce is still quite thin, you can tip your sauce into a clean saucepan and reduce over a high heat until you have the consistency you desire. Divide the pieces of lamb neck among your plates and next to it place a piece of each of the vegetables and some of the delicious sauce, then finish with a sprinkling of freshly chopped parsley.

Beef shin with dry gremolata

Serves 6–8

This recipe can be taken to the table whole, then cut and the sauce added, which is great fun as it pretty much guarantees some admiring comments. Another approach is to remove the meat from the bone after cooking, add the meat to the rich and sticky sauce, then pour it over strong, hearty pasta such as orechiette or casarecci. You can adapt this recipe to other beef cuts, such as the forequarter flank, but it is best not to use two different cuts together as they do take different times to cook. I like to serve this with a mixture of strongly flavoured greens such as cavolo nero, rocket (arugula) or silverbeet (Swiss chard) that has been simply sautéed in olive oil, chilli and garlic alongside a puddle of freshly made polenta.

For the marinade

the peel and juice of 1 orange, peel cut into strips

the peel and juice of 1 lemon, peel cut into strips

1 bunch of rosemary, leaves only

2 bay leaves

3 cloves of garlic, crushed

1 bottle of decent red wine

salt and freshly ground black pepper

For the beef

1.6–1.8 kg (3 lb 8 oz–4 lb) frenched beef shin ('frenched' basically means that your butcher has cut the top of the knuckle off)

750 ml (26 fl oz/3 cups) chicken stock (see page 74) or beef stock

6 ripe tomatoes, coarsely chopped

To make the marinade, combine the peel and juice of the orange and lemon with the rosemary leaves, bay leaves, garlic, wine and salt and pepper in a large bowl.

To prepare the beef, coat the shin with the marinade ingredients and leave for at least 2 hours, preferably overnight. Bring the meat to room temperature before cooking.

Preheat your oven to 200°C (400°F/Gas 6). Place the shin and all of the marinade in a large casserole dish or deep roasting tin. Add the stock and tomatoes (you want the liquid to come about halfway up the piece of beef), then put in the oven. What you want is to allow the beef not covered by the liquid to colour, then roll the meat over to expose the other side. Keep repeating this process every 15 minutes or so, this gives flavour and colour to your sauce and also keeps your meat moist. As the amount of liquid will reduce during cooking, pay close attention to this as you near the end of the cooking. You want a rich, sticky sauce — if you find that the sauce is reducing too far, simply add more liquid; if it is looking too watery but the beef is perfectly cooked, strain the sauce into a saucepan and reduce until you have the desired consistency. The shin should take around 2½ hours to cook.

For the dry gremolata

2 tablespoons olive oil

4 cloves of garlic, chopped

1 bunch of rosemary

1 bunch of flat-leaf (Italian) parsley

the finely grated peel of 1 orange

the finely grated peel of 1 lemon

the finely grated peel of 1 lime

150 g (5½ oz/1 cup) pine nuts,
  toasted and roughly chopped

salt

To make the dry gremolata, heat the oil in a small saucepan and fry the garlic until golden, then strain off the oil.

Remove the leaves from the rosemary and parsley and coarsely chop together. Mix the citrus peel through the herbs and spread the mixture over a piece of baking paper on a baking tray. After removing the beef from the oven reduce the heat to 150°C (300°F/Gas 2). Cover the herbs loosely with foil and cook for 20 minutes while the beef is resting, being careful not to scorch your herbs. Once your herb mix is completely dry, pound into a powder using a mortar and pestle, then combine with the pine nuts, garlic and salt.

To serve, place the beef on your serving platter and pour on some of the sauce, pouring the rest of the sauce into a jug to add to the cut meat at the table. Sprinkle a good amount of the gremolata over the beef and have some more gremolata on the table alongside the salt and pepper as an additional seasoning to be added as desired.

Gremolata is a type of spice mix that is used to flavour a meal. This recipe uses dry gremolata, which can be made in advance and stored in an airtight container or jar — it is one of those great things to have on hand as it can be used with barbecued seafood or sprinkled over meat, pasta or salads. There are many ways of drying the gremolata out completely. The nicest is to leave the mixture in direct sunshine for a couple of days. Or, if you are making it at the same time as your beef shin, follow the recipe above.

Slow-roasted pork shoulder

Serves 8–10

Here is the thing about this recipe: it takes a long, slow cook so use this to your advantage; by that I mean if you are cooking this for a Sunday dinner at say 7 o'clock, pop it in the oven while you are preparing your lunch then take the rest of the day off. Or, if you have a really full day and can't get out of that dinner you promised to cook, put this in the oven and get on with your chores. I would recommend that the first time you do this, you pick a day that you'll be home during the whole cooking process as it is in the oven for such a long time, and temperatures do differ from oven to oven, so you'll want to keep a close eye on it. When you do cook it again you'll have a better understanding of how this recipe will work in your oven and have the confidence to walk away and leave it.

2.7–3.25 kg (6 lb–7 lb 1 oz) whole pork shoulder (preferably one that has been allowed to hang for a day or so to allow the skin to dry out)
vegetable oil
salt
2 tablespoons fennel seeds
1 teaspoon chilli flakes
6 cloves of garlic, peeled
juice of 2 lemons
200 ml (7 fl oz) extra virgin olive oil

Preheat your oven to 200°C (400°F/Gas 6). To prepare the meat, pat it dry, then score the skin with a sharp knife, taking care not to cut into the flesh. Brush the pork with vegetable oil and rub a good amount of salt into the skin. Put the pork on a wire rack in a roasting tin that will be able to catch any juices. Cook in the oven until nicely coloured and the skin becomes crispy, this can take up to 1 hour. While that is happening make your paste.

Lightly toast the fennel seeds, then scoop them into a mortar and use the pestle to grind them with the chilli. Add the garlic and a little salt and keep grinding until it forms a paste. Slowly add the lemon juice and olive oil, mixing well.

Carefully remove the pork from the oven and reduce the temperature to 110°C (225°F/Gas ½). Brush the paste all over the pork. Pour a little water into the roasting tin to prevent the pan from burning. Return the pork to the oven.

Check your pork from time to time, adding a little more water to the tin if needed. You can tell when your pork is cooked when the meat starts to give from the bone when you push it with your finger — this will take between 5 and 6 hours.

I like to serve this meat with pickled coleslaw (see page 196) and some boiled potatoes.

A nice way to roast a leg of lamb

Serves 8

You'll get the best results for your roast leg of lamb if you have a roasting tin that will just fit the leg of lamb. Most butchers will cut the shank in half, which has always bugged me! Instead, stop him before he does anything silly to your lamb shank and instead ask him to cut under the shank through the back of the leg, but not all the way through so as to avoid cutting into the meat itself (another good reason to buy meat from the butcher and not the supermarket). You will still be able to fold the leg so it will fit into your tin, but the shank will stay lovely and moist and in one piece.

salt and freshly ground black pepper
1 leg of lamb, leg bone in, but hip
  bone removed, about 2.5–3 kg
  (5 lb 8 oz–6 lb 12 oz)
olive oil
1 kg (2 lb 4 oz) baby (pickling)
  onions, cut in half
2 white onions, thinly sliced
2 cloves of garlic, crushed

Preheat your oven to 190°C (375°F/Gas 5). Season the meat really well. Heat a roasting tin on top of your stove until it is nice and hot, then add a good amount of olive oil and seal and brown your meat really well. Remove the meat from the tin. Add both types of onions, the garlic cloves and cook for about 5 minutes until they start to soften. The baby onions have a good sweet flavour and keep a nice shape, while the white onions are a lot juicier and tend to almost dissolve — this will help your finished sauce to have a good consistency.

When the onions have softened, return the meat to the tin and nestle it among the onions. Cook in your preheated oven for about 1 hour and 15 minutes. During the cooking process, turn the meat a couple of times and, as the onions on top brown, stir back underneath the onions on the bottom. If you feel that the lamb and onions are colouring too quickly, splash a little water into the tin and cover with foil until the end of the cooking time. Remove the lamb from the oven and let the leg rest in the roasting tin for at least 20 minutes before serving.

Roasted lamb leg with avocado and pitta bread

Serves 8

You can use pre-made pitta bread for this recipe if you like, or make your own following the recipe on page 14; if you are going to make your own pitta I would recommend making the bread first, then the salad. You can add additional salads for feeding larger groups — try it with the pomegranate salad on page 249 and the toasted couscous and almond salad on page 279 — both wonderful additions that turn this simple meal into a great dinner party experience.

For the avocado salad

juice of 1 lime
60 ml (2 fl oz/¼ cup) sesame oil
125 ml (4 fl oz/½ cup) extra virgin olive oil
2 large red chillies, seeded and cut into thin strips
salt and freshly ground black pepper
4 ripe avocados
a few leaves of mint
a few leaves of coriander (cilantro)

For serving

1 roasted lamb leg with onions (opposite), carved
8 pitta breads (see page 14)

To make the avocado salad, place the lime juice, oils, chilli, salt and pepper in a bowl and whisk gently. Cut the avocados in half and remove the stones. Using a large tablespoon, scoop out bite-sized chunks of avocado into irregular shapes and drop them into the bowl of dressing. When all the avocado is in the bowl, add the mint and coriander leaves and fold very gently with your hands. Taste and add more seasoning if it is needed.

To serve, place your lamb in the middle of the table with the avocado salad on the side (and any other salads you are using) with a stack of pitta breads. Invite your guests to tear open one end of the pitta to make a pocket and pile in the lamb and avocado.

Veal stock

Makes 2 litres (70 fl oz/8 cups)

Making stock is very simple and an essential skill to have. Although it may seem daunting when you see recipes that require 12-hour cooking times, it is a simple case of giving it a go — when you feel comfortable with the recipes you will never buy a pre-made stock again! Pre-made stocks do not have the same 'mouthfeel' as homemade stocks and lack the rich stickiness that you get from slowly simmering bones.

   At home I collect bones from my meals, such as fish bones, beef bones and chicken bones. I chop them up (if able), wrap them up and then pop them in the freezer until I'm ready to make my stock, Sometime I'll make the stock straight away, like after roasting a chook I take off the meat and then throw the carcass into a pot with some vegetables and herbs, cover it with cold water and then let it a simmer away while I eat dinner. After I do the dishes and I strain my stock to be used another day.

5 kg (11 lb 4 oz) veal bones
½ pig trotter (get your butcher to split and freeze the other half for your next stock)
2 cloves of garlic
1 onion, chopped
3 carrots, chopped
1 celery stick, chopped
olive oil, for cooking
1 sprig of thyme
1 parsley stalk
any over-ripe tomatoes or mushroom scraps you have on hand (optional)

Preheat your oven to 200°C (400°F/Gas 6).

   Place your pig trotter in a saucepan of water, bring to the boil, then pour off the water and rinse your trotter clean. Place your bones in a roasting tray and then into a hot oven and roast them for about 30–40 minutes, or until they smell and look delicious.

   In a large frying pan, cook your garlic, onion, carrot and celery in just a dash of oil until they are tender and aromatic.

   Place all the veal bones, pig trotter, vegetables, herbs and tomatoes and mushrooms, if using, into a large saucepan or stockpot and pour in enough water to cover. Bring to a simmer but do not boil. Skim the surface to remove the scum but do not take off the fat — if your stock is on a very gentle simmer the fat will not boil through, it will sit on top of your stock and give your stock better flavour and colour; only when your stock is finished should you skim off the fat. Simmer the stock for 24 hours, topping up with cold water if required. If you are concerned about the time and don't want to cook overnight then you can take your stock off after 12 hours — it won't have the same rich flavour but will still be good.

   When you are happy with the flavour of the stock, strain and use as directed. Use within a couple of days or freeze for up to 2 months.

Veal jus

Makes 500 ml (17 fl oz/2 cups)

Veal jus is a deliciously rich, sticky and intensely flavored sauce that restaurants use to finish a dish. It is simple enough to make after roasting veal or beef if you have some homemade veal stock on hand.

2 litres (70 fl oz/8 cups) veal stock
  (see opposite)
a sprig of thyme
200 ml (7 fl oz) red wine
a dash of port (optional)
a dash of red wine vinegar
  (optional)
salt and freshly ground black pepper

Place the veal stock, meat scraps, thyme and red wine into a saucepan and bring to a simmer; skim off any scum that starts to form on the surface. Reduce your stock by three-quarters and then strain into a clean saucepan. Place back over medium heat and continue to cook the jus until you have a rich and sticky sauce. If your jus has bitter notes, then add a dash of port to sweeten. If your jus is too rich and heavy, try adding a dash of red wine vinegar to cut through the flavour. Season with salt and pepper before serving.

Fishm

Fishmonger

Taramasalata

Serves 8

There are hundreds of slightly different recipes for taramasalata. I like this one as it is well balanced and a pretty pink colour. I prefer not to use a flavoursome extra virgin olive oil in taramasalata as the taste can be too strong — instead use either a light olive oil or a mixture of 270 ml (9½ fl oz) canola oil and 80 ml (2½ fl oz/⅓ cup) extra virgin olive oil.

200 g (7 oz) very stale white bread
  with the crusts removed (don't use
  sourdough)
1 large onion, finely diced
juice of 2 lemons
salt and ground white pepper
100 g (3½ oz) tin of tarama roe
  (pasteurised red mullet roe)
350 ml (12 fl oz) light olive oil

For the adventurous, try finishing a seafood risotto with taramasalata instead of butter, or when you cook a thick chunk of blue eye cod, barramundi or other firm white fish, brush over just a little taramasalata when you rest your fish and let the flavours meld together before serving.

Break or cut the bread into chunks. Put the bread in a bowl, cover with water and soak for at least 20 minutes. When your bread has softened, squeeze out as much liquid as you can.

Depending on the size of your food processor, you may need to do this recipe in batches. If this is the case, divide everything into two and do as two different recipes, then combine both in a bowl afterwards to check for seasoning and consistency. Put the onion, lemon juice, salt and white pepper in a food processor. Blend until you have formed a paste, then add the tarama roe and blend until well combined.

Add the softened bread and continue to blend, stopping to scrape the sides of the bowl from time to time. With your food processor running, and once everything is well combined, slowly and carefully drizzle in the oil to allow the ingredients to emulsify. Once you have added all of the oil you should have a thick and creamy pinkish dip. Taste and adjust the seasoning as required — if your taramasalata is too thick you can adjust the consistency by carefully adding water a few drops at a time.

Salmon mousse with a baby herb salad

Serves 8

After much trial and error I can say with complete honesty that a good salmon mousse relies solely on good-quality salmon. I have also found that if the salmon has been too heavily brined or smoked at too high a temperature and too quickly, it will affect the oil content in the fish, which will affect the flavour and the final texture of the mousse.

For the salmon mousse
300 g (10½ oz) cold-smoked piece of salmon
a pinch of cayenne pepper
salt
220 g (7¾ oz/1 cup) thick (double/heavy) cream (or as much as you want)

For the herb salad
about 2 handfuls of mixed baby herbs
a drizzle of olive oil
a squeeze of lemon juice
salt and freshly ground black pepper
wedges of lemon, to serve

When you are making the salmon mousse you will get the best results if everything that you use to make it is very cold, so what I normally do is put the food processor bowl along with another large bowl and any utensils in the freezer for a while to chill everything.

Start by blending the smoked salmon in a food processor to a fine paste, using a rubber spatula to scrape around the inside of the bowl to ensure that it is evenly blended. While it is blending, add the cayenne pepper and salt.

Transfer the salmon purée to your chilled bowl and, using a rubber spatula, start adding the cream a little at a time, being sure to combine all of the cream before you add any more. The trick to a good mousse is to only mix it as much as you absolutely need to — if you blend the salmon too much it will start to warm up and this will change the final texture, and also if you beat the cream too much it can split and become grainy and have a nasty fatty taste. So just remember to only work it as much as you absolutely have to, which means you may not need quite as much as the recipe states.

To make the herb salad, place the herbs into a small bowl and very lightly dress with the olive oil and lemon juice. Season with salt and pepper.

To serve, I like to simply put down one nice big blob of mousse with a mound of the herb salad next to it and a couple of wedges of lemon to be squeezed over the mousse as desired. Next to this I put a few plates, a couple of knives and a pile of melba toasts (see page 297).

Kingfish swimming

Serves 10 as a starter

This dish can only be done with success when you have beautiful young ginger and fresh young coconuts. And, as the name suggests, it should always be served in a dish 'swimming' in the mild dressing made from the coconut water — you simply will not get the same results by using coconut milk or cream.

For the dressing

3 bird's eye chillies, seeds and
   stems removed
2 French shallots
1 clove of garlic, peeled
1 coriander (cilantro) root
100 g (3½ oz) shaved palm sugar
   (jaggery)
80 ml (2½ fl oz/⅓ cup) lime juice
80 ml (2½ fl oz/⅓ cup) fish sauce
1 fresh young coconut full of water,
   (make sure you give it a shake
   to hear the water sloshing about
   inside)

You can use a mortar and pestle to make the dressing, but I should warn you that it will be a bit of a workout; if you feel like taking it easy you can use a food processor. Whichever way you do it, you really need to take the time to make sure the chillies, French shallots, garlic and coriander root are completely puréed before adding the other ingredients.

Place the chillies, French shallots, garlic and coriander root into a large mortar or a food processor and smash or process until you have a fine paste. Add the palm sugar and pound or blend a little more to dissolve, then add your lime juice and fish sauce. Taste the dressing; it should be very powerful but well balanced—you want it to be hot (chilli), sweet (palm sugar), salty (fish sauce) and tart (lime juice), so add more of whatever your taste buds want. When you are happy with the flavour, pour the dressing into a bowl.

Young coconuts are relatively soft and should pose no problems to get into them. Use the heel of a large chopping knife and carefully start to hack a circle into the top of the coconut until you are able to lift off the top. Stir the dressing while you slowly pour in the coconut water until you have a nice soft dressing — remember that you want the kingfish to be 'swimming' in the dressing so you don't want the flavour to be too strong. Now use a large spoon to scoop out the soft silky flesh of the coconut and place onto a chopping board, and then slice into very thin strips.

For the kingfish

1 whole fillet of kingfish,
  900 g–1.1 kg
(2 lb–2 lb 7 oz)

For serving

4 cm (1 ½ inch) long piece of
  fresh ginger
1 large red chilli
2 avocados
a few leaves of coriander (cilantro)
  and mint

 I normally buy a whole fillet of Hiramasa kingfish that weighs 900 g (2 lb), which is ideal for about 10 people for a starter; if you want to serve it as a main meal, then you should double the recipe. As you will be serving the kingfish raw, take care to purchase the best and freshest fish you can find.

To skin the kingfish fillet, place the kingfish, skin side down and lengthways along your chopping board. Position a sharp knife just up from the tail of the fillet and make a small cut across the fillet down to the skin, but not through the skin. Position the fillet so that you can take a firm grasp of the little cut piece of flesh at the tail in one hand, then slide the knife under the fillet but above the skin of the fish.

The next stage should be done in as clean a motion as you can. Angle the blade of your knife slightly towards the skin and apply just a little downward pressure as you slice along the fish using a slow sawing motion — the skin should come away in one piece but any little pieces of skin left behind can be removed later. You can do the above or you can buy some slices of kingfish sashimi from your local sushi restaurant, but I reckon this takes out a lot of the fun of this dish.

To serve, I like the kingfish to be presented as individual little mouthfuls that are soaked in the dressing, so I usually either place each piece of fish on a skewer or serve with a little glass of toothpicks or short skewers nearby.

Take your ginger and peel it, then cut into nice thin strips. Take the chilli and cut in half lengthways, scrape out the seeds and cut into thin strips. Cut your avocados in half and remove the stones. Now take your kingfish and cut into thin slices across the fillet.

To serve, use a platter or plate with a high lip. Use a teaspoon to scoop out chunks of the avocado and arrange on the platter. Drape a piece of kingfish over each piece of avocado. Top this with the strips of ginger and chilli, then scatter over the leaves of coriander and mint before pouring the dressing over each little pile. Serve immediately.

Potted prawns with frisée and chive salad

Serves 8–10

This is something you can make up to a week in advance and have ready to simply drop on the table when everyone is ready. Though it is very rich, it is a delicious way to start a meal. I have changed the basic flavours of the classic recipe slightly to make it more aromatic, which helps when eating a big serve of butter.

1 kg (2 lb 4 oz) very fresh school prawns (shrimp)
300 g (10½ oz) butter
2 star anise
6 bay leaves
4 green cardamom pods, cracked open
a generous pinch of cracked white pepper
a generous pinch of salt

Blanch the prawns in water on a rolling boil for about 2 minutes, then plunge into iced water. Drain, then start to peel, putting the peeled prawns into a bowl. This may seem a little daunting as school prawns are tiny and fiddly, but there is a trick to it — most of the shell is soft enough to eat, so all you need to remove are the harder parts of the prawn (that is, the head, legs and tail). And don't forget to daydream while doing this.

While you are peeling, put the butter and all of the other ingredients in a saucepan over a very low heat to allow the flavours to infuse. After about 30 minutes (which should be long enough to peel the prawns), strain off the solids from the butter and put the butter in the fridge to cool a little.

When the butter is cool (but not set; if the butter sets, melt it again), pour the butter over the prawns and gently stir. Taste the prawns and check for seasoning — you want them to be well seasoned, almost too salty, as this is going to be served cold. Pour the prawns into ramekins or one dish that is just big enough to fit all of the prawns snugly, then pour over all of the butter. You want the prawns to be covered by the butter, so poke down any rogue bits — you may even have to melt a little more butter. Refrigerate for at least 3 hours.

Remove from the fridge about 40 minutes before you want to serve, or just long enough to take off the chill.

For the frisée and chive salad

100 g (3½ oz) French shallots,
  finely chopped
a pinch of salt
a pinch of sugar
freshly ground black pepper
80 ml (2½ fl oz/⅓ cup) white vinegar
3 heads of frisée (curly endive)
200 ml (7 fl oz) extra virgin olive oil
1 bunch of chives, finely snipped

For serving

toast
a few wedges of lime, optional

To make the frisée and chive salad, put the shallots in a small bowl and season with the salt, sugar, pepper and vinegar. Leave to sit for about 20 minutes to allow the shallots to pickle slightly. Meanwhile, carefully remove the bitter tough outside dark green leaves of the frisée and reserve the golden to pale green inner leaves. Whisk the oil into the shallot mixture and check the seasoning. Add your leaves and chives and toss well.

To serve, place the dish of prawns on a platter (or individual plates) alongside the salad, and serve with some toast and perhaps some lime wedges. Provide a couple of bread knives to make it easier to eat.

Boiled crab with lime butter

Serves 4

I first cooked this recipe with friends on the beach in San Quentin, Baja California. We had one bowl, a campfire, and a cool box for a fridge, so if we could make the recipe work there I am guessing that you should be able to pull it off anywhere. You can use mud crabs or blue swimmer crabs, but if you can get them, mud crabs are better.

For the lime butter
125 g (4½ oz) butter
3 limes
½ bunch of coriander (cilantro)
3 large red chillies (keep the seeds in if you like things hot)
a drizzle of honey
salt and freshly ground black pepper

For the crab
2 x 600–800 g (1 lb 5 oz–1 lb 12 oz) whole live crabs (either mud crabs or blue swimmer crabs)
sea water (if you happen to have it on hand) or water seasoned really well with mineral salts or sea salt
coriander (cilantro) leaves, to serve

To make the lime butter, soften the butter slightly and whisk it in a bowl until it is white and creamy. Grate the lime peel, then squeeze the limes so you get all the juice. Chop all of the coriander except for the root. Remove the seeds and membrane from the chilli, then dice the flesh. Add all of the ingredients to the bowl with the butter and keep mixing together until really well incorporated. Taste for seasoning.

To make the crab, bring a large pot of water to a rapid boil — you need a large pot or the water temperature will drop too much when you add the crabs. I prefer to kill crab by using a heavy knife, a keen eye and a firm hand — drive the tip of your knife into the top of the head, just above and in between the eyes, then cut all the way through in one swift movement; this will kill the crab instantly. I prefer this to any slow killing such as freezing, drowning or just plain boiling as I believe it is better for the crab, better for the meat (as there is no time for shock to damage the flesh) and better for my conscience. Cook the crab in the pot of rapidly boiling water for 12 minutes, then take out of the pot and rest for 6 minutes before serving.

When you are ready to serve, remove the head by taking a firm grip on the crab, and with your other hand lift the side of the head up and away. Remove the gills (sometimes known as dead man's fingers); these are the brown–grey strips that lay on either side of the head. Using the back of a heavy knife or a hammer, crack the shell, but keep it intact, then place the crab in a large bowl and toss in some of the butter — allow the flavours to settle in. Sprinkle with coriander and serve while still hot with a dish of sea salt and the rest of the butter in a little pot.

Seared scallops with steamed artichoke butter

Serves 4

Allow as many scallops in their shell as you want for each person. For each scallop you will need about 1 teaspoon of butter. This recipe depends on how much artichoke purée you can yield from your artichoke — don't stress if you end up with too much; just put it into the fridge and use at a later date — it will keep quite well for 2–3 weeks.

For the steamed artichoke butter
4 artichokes
1 lemon
a pinch of salt and freshly ground
  black pepper
a dash of honey
about 250 g (9 oz) butter

For the scallops
scallops in the shell
vegetable oil, optional

If fresh artichokes are out of season, you can use 120 g (4¼ oz/ heaped ½ cup) of drained good-quality artichokes in olive oil.

To make the artichoke butter, put the artichokes in a steamer basket over a saucepan of simmering water until tender when pierced with a knife (for large artichokes you'll need 25–30 minutes). Allow to cool completely. Keep removing the leaves of the artichoke until you reach the yellow, tender leaves. Place an artichoke on its side; you should be able to see where the leaves finish and the heart begins. Using a sharp serrated knife cut off the leaves. Working carefully, use a sharp paring knife or small vegetable knife to trim away the dark green exterior of the artichoke. Cut the stem about 2 cm (¾ inches) down from the base of the heart. Using a spoon, scrape out all of the spiky 'choke' from the centre of the heart. Rinse under cold water, then rub the heart well with a piece of cut lemon to stop it from turning brown. Repeat with the other artichokes. Using a fork, mash the artichoke heart into a bowl. Grate over a little lemon peel, then add a pinch of salt and a dash of honey. In a separate bowl whisk about the same amount of butter as you have artichoke purée and keep mixing until it is creamed. Add the butter to the artichoke purée and whisk until well combined. Taste for seasoning.

If you are cooking a lot of scallops, place a dollop (about 1 heaped teaspoon) of steamed artichoke butter on each scallop and place under a very hot grill (broiler); they will take no more than 2 minutes to cook. Alternatively, if you are only cooking a few, you can fry the scallops. First remove them from their shells, reserving the shells, place into a bowl and drizzle with a little oil. Heat a frying pan until very hot and when the scallops are golden on the bottom, add a generous dollop of the butter to the pan. When the butter starts to melt, turn the scallops over. Lift each scallop onto a shell and spoon over some of the butter. Serve immediately.

Preserved octopus salad with olives and fennel

Serves 8

The type of octopus available to you will depend on where you live and what is available at the fishmarkets. Baby octopus is readily available but I prefer not to use it for this recipe. If, however, that is all you can get, cut the octopus into larger pieces, or even just in half, and pay really close attention as they will overcook quite easily.

For the octopus

2 kg (4 lb 8 oz) giant octopus
1 tablespoon coriander seeds
1 teaspoon fennel seeds
¼ teaspoon chilli flakes
freshly ground black pepper
1 litre (35 fl oz/4 cups) olive oil
   (not extra virgin)
300 ml (10½ fl oz) dry white wine
150 g (5½ oz/about ¾ cup) olives,
   such as kalamata, ligurian or
   manzanella
4 stalks of celery, finely diced
½ head of fennel, finely diced
6 cloves of garlic, crushed
2 large red chillies, split and seeded
1 lemon, peeled, peel reserved
4 bay leaves
lemon juice or white vinegar
   (optional)

Start by cleaning the octopus in plenty of cold water and give it a really good scrub, then remove from the water and pat dry with a clean cloth. Place the octopus onto your chopping board and remove the head by cutting just above the tentacles. Carefully slice up the back of the head, take a firm grip and open the head sac up and remove all the guts, then rinse the head clean. Cut the head in half. Now remove the beak from the middle of the legs and cut the legs into pieces about 10 cm (4 inches) long.

Place the octopus pieces in a bowl with the coriander and fennel seeds, chilli flakes and plenty of black pepper. Choose a large, high-sided saucepan that will comfortably fit all the ingredients — they should only come about halfway up the pan; this will eliminate the chance of any oil boiling over during cooking. Heat the oil in the pan over a high heat and, when the oil is very hot, very carefully lower in the octopus pieces, taking care not to let the oil boil over. When the octopus is in the pan it will cool the oil down; keep the heat on high and stir the octopus from time to time. As the temperature increases and the moisture is cooked out, the octopus will start to fry again, about 20–30 minutes. You will know it is frying because the oil starts to sound different.

When this happens, carefully add the wine a splash at a time at first to avoid the oil boiling over. When you have added all of the wine, keep cooking on a high heat until almost all of the wine has evaporated. You will be able to tell this because when you first start cooking the wine the oil will look quite milky, but as the wine cooks out, the oil will start to become clear. Now add the olives, celery, fennel, garlic, chillies, lemon peel and bay leaves and stir really well. Keep the pan on a high temperature and keep cooking until the vegetables and octopus feel tender when tested with the tip of a knife. Depending on the size of the octopus this last stage

For the salad

1 head of fennel

1 lemon

1 handful of flat-leaf (Italian)
 parsley, coarsely chopped

For serving

olive oil, optional

salt and freshly ground black pepper

can take anywhere from 5–30 minutes — when checking the octopus, choose one of the large pieces. Taste some of the octopus and adjust the seasoning if needed; you can also add a splash of lemon juice or white vinegar to the octopus if you prefer a more 'pickled' flavour.

The octopus is now ready to serve straight away but its flavour is nicer if left for a couple of days in the oil in the fridge. If you do want to keep this longer than a few days, then simply place everything into a sterilised jar (you'll need one that has about a 1.5 litre/52 fl oz/6-cup capacity) and ensure that everything is completely covered with oil — any bits poking out will become mouldy and go off quite quickly. This will keep in the fridge for up to 3 weeks.

To make the salad, shave the fennel into a bowl, then add a tiny bit of grated lemon zest, the juice from the lemon and the parsley.

To serve, remove the octopus from the oil, slice as thinly as possible and place in the bowl with the fennel. Use a slotted spoon to collect some of the cooked vegetables from the octopus oil. There should be enough oil on the octopus and the vegetables to dress the salad, but if not, simply add a little more. Add a little more salt and pepper and gently toss the salad and serve immediately.

Sardine and bean salad

Serves 4

When you make this salad buy whatever fresh beans look best on the day. I use a selection of juicy, yellow butterbeans, thick crunchy roman beans and delicate baby green beans, broad beans, sugar snap peas and snow peas.

For the green bean salad
250 g (9 oz) yellow butterbeans
 (lima beans)
150 g (5½ oz) baby green beans
150 g (5½ oz) roman beans
500 g (1 lb 2 oz) broad (fava) beans
 in the pod
100 g (3½ oz) sugar snap peas
100 g (3½ oz) snow peas
 (mangetout)
1 portion of tomato dressing
 (see page 228)
a few torn basil leaves

For the grilled sardines
12 sardine fillets, butterflied
4 tablespoons tomato base
 (see page 228) or tomato paste
 (concentrated purée)

For serving
a scattering of herbed breadcrumbs
 (see note page 297)

To make the green bean salad, I like to pinch the stem off the butterbeans and green beans, but leave the tail attached. Use a knife to 'grab' the top of the roman beans and pull out the vein, then repeat on the other end. Cut into 1 cm (½ inch) long diamonds. Remove the broad beans from the pod. Using a knife, grab the stem of the sugar snap peas and the snow peas and pull off the vein and repeat for the other side. I like to julienne the snow peas and cut the sugar snaps in half lengthways.

As each of the beans cooks at different rates, I recommend cooking them separately, then removing with a slotted spoon and rapidly cooling under cold water. You can use the same pot of water to cook all the beans, making sure to keep it on the boil. Cook the broad beans last as they will discolour your water. Cook the butterbeans for 4 minutes, the baby beans for 2–3 minutes, the roman beans for 5–6 minutes and the broad beans for no more than 2 minutes. Once the broad beans are cooked, cool, then squeeze each one out of the pale green skin to reveal the brilliant green bean. Leave the sugar snap peas and snow peas raw. Combine all of the beans in the bowl with the tomato dressing and torn basil and leave it to sit for a couple of minutes.

To grill the sardines, brush a little of the tomato base over each side, then cook, skin side up, under a very hot grill (broiler) for 5 minutes or cook on a hot barbecue, skin side down, for 3–4 minutes.

To serve, arrange the salad on four plates and then top with the cooked sardines. Scatter with the breadcrumbs.

Steamed oysters with green onion pickle

Serves 2–4

For the green onion pickle
200 ml (7 fl oz) vegetable oil
280 g (10 oz) caster (superfine)
  sugar
6 bunches spring onions (scallions),
  chopped
a small knob of ginger, grated
white vinegar, to taste

For the oysters
24 oysters, on the half-shell

To make the green onion pickle, place the oil and sugar in a heavy-based saucepan over high heat and stir and until the sugar starts to fry into a weird clumpy caramel. When it's the colour of straw, add the onion, ginger and vinegar and continue to cook for a couple of minutes, then remove from the heat and allow to cool in the pan — this will ensure any clumps of caramel will dissolve into the pickle. When it has cooled, taste and adjust the seasoning as required. Green onion pickle can be kept in an airtight container in the refrigerator for up to 2 weeks.

Before you cook your oysters, get your steamer nice and hot. Place your oysters in the steamer and cook for as little as possible, just enough to warm them through — small oysters may take 45 seconds, larger pacific oysters could take up to 2 minutes. Once the oysters are cooked, tip off any excess liquid and arrange on a platter, then carefully spoon just a little green onion pickle on top of each.

Blue eye cod in clam chowder

Serves 4

I adapted this chowder dish from a recipe that I discovered was written in 1751, which makes note of a technique I have tried to mimic, called 'chowder layering technique'. It is different from most other recipes I have seen and is a great dish to share.

For the croutons
6 slices of stale white bread
3 tablespoons butter, melted

For the chowder
120 g (4¼ oz) smoky bacon, chopped
a knob of butter
1 large white onion, peeled and finely diced
1 clove of garlic, chopped
2 tablespoons plain (all-purpose) flour
½ teaspoon smoky paprika
500 ml (17 fl oz/2 cups) milk
300 ml (10½ fl oz) fish stock or water
200 ml (7 fl oz) cream
1 large desiree or other all-purpose potato, peeled and cut into dice the size of a pea
1 bunch of thyme
2 bay leaves
a couple of sprigs of marjoram
a couple of sprigs of oregano
freshly ground black pepper
1 piece of blue eye cod, about 800 g (1 lb 12 oz), skin removed (avoid the tail piece to ensure even cooking)
24 large clams or about 40 vongole (baby clams), purged (see note)
a sprinkle of chopped flat-leaf (Italian) parsley, to serve

Preheat your oven to 190°C (375°F/Gas 5). To make the croutons, remove the crusts from the bread and cut the bread into small cubes. Place in a bowl, drizzle with butter and mix. Put on a baking tray, then bake for about 5 minutes until golden and crunchy.

To make the chowder, I like to use a wide flat flameproof casserole dish that will comfortably take all of your ingredients (it needs to have a lid). Place your bacon into the bottom of your cold casserole dish and add a knob of butter, place on a low heat and allow the fat to render out of the bacon, while letting the bacon take on a nice brown colour — this should take about 5 minutes. When you are happy with the colour of the bacon, remove the meat from the dish, leaving as much of the fat in the dish as possible, then add the onion and garlic. Cook this until the onion is nice and soft, then add the flour and paprika and cook this mixture for another 5 minutes or so.

Add the liquids a little at a time to avoid any lumps forming. When all the liquid has been incorporated, add the diced potato, thyme, bay, marjoram, oregano and a really good grinding of black pepper but hold back on the salt for now as the clams will add their own saltiness. Once you have a gentle simmer, carefully add the cod in one piece, then place the clams around the fish — the fillet should be just covered with liquid, but it doesn't matter if the clams are not completely covered. Cover with the lid.

When buying the clams ask if they have been purged; if not, when you get home simply cover the clams with cold tap water, add a little salt and leave in your fridge for at least 8–10 hours but no longer than 24 hours. This will give them time to open up and flush fresh water through to remove any grit and sand.

Move the chowder ingredients about from time to time to make sure that everything is cooking evenly. What will happen is the clams will steam open, releasing their juices and the cooking cod will also be flavouring the soup. You want to take care not to overcook the fish; you actually want to turn off the heat just before the fish is cooked, as it is going to remain in the liquid and will continue to keep cooking. The cooking time depends on the thickness of your fillet: a basic rule of thumb is to cook for 8–12 minutes, then check your fish by pushing with your finger or a spoon. Blue eye cod and other thick flaky white fish will feel almost bouncy just before it is cooked — if you experiment on a raw piece of fish you will know what I mean. Raw fish feels almost hard, nearly cooked will feel bouncy, and overcooked will feel spongy and dry.

Serve the chowder at the table with a scattering of parsley and the croutons — you will need to serve it with a ladle and a pair of tongs.

Barbecued cuttlefish and crispy pancetta with a chilli zucchini and a tahini dressing

Serves 4

If you have never eaten cuttlefish before, then make a point of trying it. At first glance you may think that cuttlefish looks just like squid, and it is in fact very similar — if you have trouble finding cuttlefish you can substitute squid. My preference for cuttlefish stems from the fact that I prefer its 'crunchy' texture.

For the chilli zucchini dressing
4 zucchini (courgettes)
2 cloves of garlic, crushed
2 large red chillies, seeded and
  finely chopped
185 ml (6 fl oz/¾ cup) olive oil
salt and freshly ground black pepper

For the crispy pancetta
8 pieces of pancetta (see note)

For the tahini dressing
2½ tablespoons tahini
1½ tablespoons lemon juice
salt and freshly ground black pepper
water
sugar (optional)

To make the zucchini dressing, dice the zucchini — I find the easiest way to do this is to slice it lengthways on a mandolin first, then cut the zucchini into strips and, finally, into small dice. This is a little fiddly but the result is well worth it.

In a bowl, combine your zucchini, garlic and chilli, then heat a little of your oil in a large frying pan over medium–high heat and fry some of the zucchini. You want to cook your zucchini until it is a beautiful golden colour, which will give an amazing sweet flavour to your dressing; when you are cooking the zucchini you don't want to have too much in the pan at a time, so it may pay to cook it in batches unless you have a very large frying pan. When you have a nice light brown colour on the zucchini, transfer it to a clean bowl, wipe out the pan and repeat the process until all the zucchini is cooked. Season with salt and pepper.

Preheat your oven to 180°C (350°F/Gas 4). To make the crispy pancetta, lay out the pancetta on a baking tray lined with baking paper and bake for about 10 minutes, or until crispy. Carefully lift your pancetta onto paper towel to drain.

To make the tahini dressing, put the tahini in a bowl, then whisk in the lemon juice, salt and pepper. As soon as you start to incorporate liquid into tahini, it will thicken — adjust the consistency with water until it resembles pouring cream. I really like the bitter flavour of tahini, but if you prefer you can sweeten with sugar.

For the cuttlefish
16 even-sized cuttlefish
vegetable oil
salt and freshly ground black pepper

For serving
a few leaves of mint
about 100 ml (3½ fl oz) verjuice

Make sure that you buy 'flat pancetta' that is sliced to order. What I have found is that pre-sliced pancetta can dry out and may taste a little dull — there should be more to the flavour of pancetta than just that of salty pork.

If you don't mind cleaning fish, then I would recommend that you buy whole cuttlefish and clean them when you get home as you'll get a better result. However, if you prefer, you can ask your fish supplier to clean it for you. To clean the cuttlefish, take the body in one hand and the legs in the other and use a gentle pulling motion to remove the legs and innards. Use your fingers to pull out the remaining guts. Take the body of the cuttlefish in your hands and use your thumb to push out the bone and then, using a dry tea towel (dish towel) to help you get a grip of the skin, gently peel away the skin. Rinse the cuttlefish under cold running water, then pat dry. Repeat the process with the rest of the cuttlefish.

Take your cleaned cuttlefish and, with a sharp knife, very carefully make shallow slashes across the cuttlefish, then give it a quarter turn and cut across the first cuts so that the cuttlefish has tiny little squares cut into it. Place all of your cuttlefish into a bowl and drizzle with a little oil and season really well. Place the cuttlefish onto a hot barbecue or grill plate and cook for about 1½ minutes on one side and 30–40 seconds on the other.

To serve, put the cooked cuttlefish in a clean bowl with your chilli zucchini dressing, mint leaves and the verjuice and combine really well. Arrange the cuttlefish on a platter and drizzle with the tahini dressing, then arrange the pieces of pancetta over the top.

Smoked eel with potato and bacon salad

Serves 8

1 whole smoked eel (these are usually between 875 g–1 kg/ 1 lb 15 oz–2 lb 4 oz), fillets removed and skin and backbone discarded

1 bunch of watercress, picked and washed

1 small piece of fresh horseradish or a couple of spoonfuls of pickled horseradish

8 pieces of smoked bacon

16 small cooked cocktail potatoes, cut in half

lemon juice, to taste

250 ml (9 fl oz/1 cup) extra virgin olive oil

½ bunch of flat-leaf (Italian) parsley, leaves coarsely chopped

salt and freshly ground black pepper

This is a warm salad, which means that you want to cook and serve it straight away, so you will need to make sure that you have all of your ingredients ready to go. Halve the eel lengthways and cut into 6 cm (2½ inch) batons. Set aside. Put the watercress in a large bowl and have ready a fine grater to grate the horseradish to finish off the salad. Cut the bacon into pieces that are roughly the same size as the eel, then put them in a large frying pan over a medium heat and cook until they start to go crispy. Turn and cook the other side. When the bacon is cooked, lift it out of the pan and put to one side, but be sure not to discard any of the bacon fat — you want to use this as part of the dressing.

Add the potatoes to the pan and move them about just enough to warm them, then turn off the heat and gently add the pieces of eel just long enough to warm them. Squeeze in your lemon juice, add the olive oil and chopped parsley and season really well. Now tip everything into the bowl with the watercress and, using a wooden spoon or your hands, carefully fold all of the ingredients together. Grate on as much of the horseradish as you want and mix again. Arrange your salad on a platter, top with your pieces of bacon and then finish with a little more grated horseradish.

Baked vongole with bruschetta

Serves 4

Vongole is the name given to baby clams, and the beauty of vongole is that they are tiny sweet explosions of flavour. Just remember that when you buy vongole you should ask whether or not they have been 'purged' to remove the gritty sand. If not, it is an easy thing to do yourself, and I have included the instructions on page 161.

For the bruschetta

4–8 thick slices of sourdough bread
olive oil, for drizzling
salt and freshly ground black pepper
a couple of cloves of garlic

For the baked vongole

40 vongole, purged (see note
 page 161)
2 tomatoes, peeled, halved and
 seeded
2 cloves of garlic
55 ml (1¾ fl oz) extra virgin olive oil
125 ml (4 fl oz/½ cup) dry white
 wine
1 bunch of thyme
1 bay leaf
salt and freshly ground black pepper

Preheat the oven to 180°C (350°F/Gas 4). To make the bruschetta, simply drizzle the bread with a little olive oil and season before placing on a baking tray and baking until the bread is nice and golden, rub each piece with a little of the raw garlic. Keep warm while cooking the vongole.

To make the baked vongole, rinse off your purged vongole. You want to wrap the vongole in a double layer of foil, so lay out a sheet that you feel will be big enough to take the vongole and then lay out another sheet over the top. Tip on the vongole and all the other ingredients, taking care not to let the liquids spill out. Now wrap up the vongole into a foil parcel; when you are wrapping, make sure that you leave enough room for the clams to open up comfortably.

Place a dry frying pan onto a high heat and, when it is good and hot, add the vongole parcel and push down a little to ensure the parcel is fitting snuggly on the bottom of the pan. When you start to see steam coming out of the parcel, continue to cook for about another 5 minutes, shaking the pan from time to time to ensure even cooking (as if you were making popcorn). Remove the pan from the heat and transfer the whole parcel, unopened, to a platter.

Serve immediately by placing the platter in the middle of your group. Use a pair of scissors to cut open the foil parcel — take care though as the foil will cool very quickly and may not feel hot to touch, but inside a good head of steam is just waiting to burst out. Serve with the bruschetta.

Danks Street prawn cocktail

Serves 6

You'll need a mouli for this recipe — it is the best thing to 'squeeze' the flavour out of the prawn shells. It is a great piece of equipment that every well-equipped kitchen needs and its use helps to make this dish really shine.

For the prawns
a handful of good-quality salt (I like sel gris from France or pink salt from the Murray Basin in Victoria)
about 1 kg (2 lb 4 oz) large raw prawns (shrimp)
iced water

For the cocktail sauce
50 g (1¾ oz) butter
a few sprigs of thyme
2 cloves of garlic
1 strip of orange peel
1 tablespoon orange juice
3 ripe tomatoes, chopped
80 ml (2½ fl oz /⅓ cup) brandy
1 large red chilli, split and seeded
125 g (4½ oz/½ cup) mayonnaise (see page 75)
salt and freshly ground black pepper

For serving
iceberg lettuce
6 lemon wedges

To cook the prawns, bring a large saucepan of water to the boil and add the salt. Boil the prawns for as little time as you can — large prawns will take 3–5 minutes. Plunge the prawns into iced water until completely chilled.

Clean the prawns by removing the head and peeling the shell away from the body, but leave the tail on; you may wish to devein them. Keep all the heads and shells for the sauce.

To make the cocktail sauce, melt the butter in a large saucepan, then add your reserved prawn heads and shells, the thyme and garlic. Cook this until the butter and prawns brown slightly, then add all of the remaining ingredients except the mayonnaise. Turn down the heat of your pan so everything stews nice and slowly. After 15–20 minutes of cooking and occasional stirring, your mixture should start to get a little dry, but if it is too dry add a little water — you want your mixture to look juicy but not too wet.

Now take everything and push as much as you can through a mouli to extract a concentrated paste. Allow to cool slightly then mix this paste through the mayonnaise. Taste and adjust the seasoning — you are looking for a nice, powerful prawn cocktail sauce with just a hint of chilli.

To serve, cut a big fat wedge of iceberg lettuce, pile your prawns on top of that, then add a dollop of the cocktail sauce. Serve with lemon wedges.

Whole poached salmon

Serves 10

To poach a salmon you really need only two things. The first, a fish. The second, a pan that will fit the fish comfortably — you do not want your fish to be bent in the pan, it must remain flat. The choice of poaching liquid is up to you — if you have a nice fresh fish stock use that, otherwise use the following poaching liquid.

7 litres (245 fl oz /28 cups) water
1 litre (35 fl oz /4 cups) dry white
  wine
1½ bunches of flat-leaf (Italian)
  parsley
1½ lemons, sliced
1½ stalks of celery
1½ onions, cut into quarters
salt and freshly ground black pepper
3 kg (6 lb 12 oz) whole salmon that
  has been gutted and scaled
chopped herbs, optional
caper and egg dressing, to serve
  (see page 73)

One 3 kg (6 lb 12 oz) salmon will feed ten people. If you don't have the luxury of a large pan, you can easily refine this recipe to cook individual portions of salmon by poaching in the same liquid. A piece of fish that weighs 165 g (5¾ oz) will take 4–5 minutes when cooked on a gentle simmer. Or, if it is steamed it will take 5–6 minutes.

Place the water, wine, parsley, lemon, celery, onion and salt and pepper in a pot that is large enough to fit the fish without it being bent. Bring the poaching liquid to the boil and gently simmer for about 15 minutes, which is just long enough to blend all the flavours together. Gently lower in the fish and ensure that it is completely covered. Do not let the liquid boil; just simmer very gently. A fish of this size will take around 20–22 minutes of cooking. Take the pot off the heat and allow your fish to cool completely before removing from the poaching liquid.

If you have never served a whole fish like this before now, take a deep breath and relax; it is not difficult and there is nothing to worry about. Sure, it may seem a little daunting, but there really is nothing to it. Remove the fish from the poaching liquid and very carefully remove the skin from the top fillet. Using a rubber spatula in each hand (or simply your hands), very carefully start to lift the top fillet away from the fish, then place on a board. Now, take hold of the head and gently pull up and backwards towards the tail — you should be able to remove the head, spine, all the bones and the tail in one easy go, then any stray bones can be easily picked out. Using the spatulas again, remove the bottom fillet, leaving the skin behind. Place the bottom fillet on a serving platter, season the fillet with plenty of salt and pepper and, if you wish, sprinkle on some chopped herbs, such as parsley, chervil or chives. Place the top fillet back to present the 'whole' fish. Serve with the caper and egg dressing on the side.

Linguine with spanner crab and prawn butter

serves 4

I love this prawn butter recipe because 90 per cent of Australians are expert at completing the first step, which is consuming a pile of cooked prawns and and then sealing the peeled shells and heads in a plastic bag and freezing them. Most people do this so the bin doesn't get smelly before rubbish day, but I would beg of you to keep them and try to make this simple recipe to produce a delicious, rich and aromatic butter that can be used in so many ways. It can be stirred through pasta or fish soups or brushed over fish, among other things.

For the Prawn Butter
splash of olive oil
300 g (10½ oz) butter, cut into
  large pieces
1 large carrot, finely diced
1 small red onion, finely diced
½ celery stalk, finely diced
2 garlic cloves, peeled
1 large fresh red chilli
1 small knob of ginger
1 star anise
1 teaspoon coriander seeds
½ bunch thyme, leaves picked
2 bay leaves
salt and freshly ground pepper
500 g (1 lb 2 oz) boiled prawn shells
  and heads
splash of brandy (if you have it)

Heat a little oil into a large saucepan and add a knob of the butter. When the butter is foaming, add the carrot, onion, celery, garlic, chilli, ginger, spices and herbs to the pan and season with salt and pepper. Stir occasionally until the vegetables have started to colour.

Add the prawn shells, stir well to combine, and cook for another 10 minutes, or until the prawns release a delicious aroma. Use a wooden spoon to stir the mixture and crush the shells as they cook. If you are adding the brandy, do so now but be careful, as it may flame up for a second. If it does, don't panic — the flames will subside very quickly as the alcohol cooks out of the liquor.

Add the remaining butter to the pan in large chunks, reduce the heat to very low, and cook for about 20 minutes, stirring until all the butter has melted. While the butter is still hot, pour the mixture through a mouli on the finest setting. If you don't have a mouli, push as much of the mixture as you can through a fine sieve; using a sieve will give you less yield but still a good result. Remove to a container and refrigerate until set. The butter will set on the top and solids will set on the bottom. Scrape the butter off the top, discard the solids.

The butter is now ready to use, but if you want to keep it for a while, place it in a saucepan and bring to the boil. While it's still hot, pour it into a sterilised jar, then allow to cool completely, seal and refrigerate for up to 3 weeks.

For the linguine with spanner crab

320 g (11¼ oz) linguine

125 ml (4 fl oz/½ cup) extra virgin
  olive oil

200 g (7 oz) cooked spanner
  crabmeat

juice of 1 lemon

salt and freshly ground pepper

1 bunch mint, leaves chopped

1 bunch flat-leaf (Italian) parsley,
  leaves chopped

2 large fresh red chillies, seeded
  and chopped

Cook the pasta in a large saucepan of salted boiling water until al dente. Drain and set aside.

Heat the olive oil in a large frying pan over medium–high heat so that it is hot but not smoking. Add the crabmeat, lemon juice, salt and pepper. Stir with a spatula to break the crab up through the oil — you should have a loose mixture; if it's too firm for your liking, add more oil. Add the pasta and toss to combine over very gentle heat until well combined and heated through. Add the mint, parsley and chilli, to taste, and mix it all up some more. Add some of the prawn butter, to taste, season with salt and pepper and serve straight away.

Casserole of pork belly, pancetta and clams

Serves 8

I know this sounds like a pretty crazy combination but it works incredibly well. There is a little bit of preparation involved and you have to start the day before. When you look over the recipe you will see that it also involves marinating the pork in milk overnight, but please don't be put off — take a chance and you won't be disappointed.

For the pork belly

1 kg (2 lb 4 oz) piece of pork belly
  off the bone, skin removed
100 ml (3½ fl oz) dry white wine
500 ml (17 fl oz/2 cups) milk
4 bay leaves
salt and freshly ground black pepper

For the potatoes

6 (about 750 g/1 lb 10 oz) pontiac
  potatoes or sweet waxy potatoes
olive oil
salt and freshly ground black pepper
1 bulb of garlic, unpeeled, cut in
  half crossways
a few sprigs of thyme
2 bay leaves

For the tomatoes

8 ripe roma (plum) tomatoes
salt and freshly ground black pepper
a drizzle of olive oil
1 clove of garlic, crushed

Take the pork belly and cut it into 1.5 cm (⅝ inch) cubes and place it in a bowl with the white wine, milk, bay leaves and a little salt and a good grinding of black pepper. Cover with plastic wrap and let it sit in the fridge overnight.

Preheat your oven to 180°C (450°F/Gas 4). To make the potatoes, place the potatoes on a roasting tray, drizzle with a little olive oil, season with salt and pepper and add your garlic, thyme and bay leaves. Cover with foil and bake for about 50 minutes, or until the potatoes are tender when tested with a knife. Remove the potatoes from the oven and lift off the foil. Discard the garlic, thyme and bay leaves. They can now be stored in the fridge overnight, if you want to prepare them earlier, or you can continue with the next step straight away.

Use the back of a spoon to squash the potatoes flat so that they almost cover the whole pan. Add a little more olive oil, place the roasting tray on your stovetop over two hobs and start to gently fry on a gentle heat. When they are well coloured, turn them over and fry the other side — this will take about 20–30 minutes in total and you may need to add a little more oil. Set aside.

To make the tomatoes, cut them in half and place on a roasting tray, cut side down. Season with a little salt and pepper, drizzle with a little olive oil and add the garlic.

For the casserole

a good slug of olive oil

185 g (6½ oz) pancetta, cut into
  lardons (short batons)

3 cloves of garlic, crushed

8 French shallots, thinly sliced

1.5 kg (3 lb 5 oz) surf clams or
  vongole, purged of grit
  (see note page 161)

200 ml (7 fl oz) vermouth

350 ml (12 fl oz) chicken stock

1 bunch of thyme

a sprinkling of chopped flat-leaf
  (Italian) parsley

To start the casserole you need to drain off the pork belly, rinse it really well and then pat dry. Now place a large flameproof casserole dish onto the top of your stove on a high heat and pour in a good slug of olive oil. When the oil is nice and hot, add your pieces of pork. Fry the pork in batches for a while to get a good brown colour, turning the pieces from time to time. Transfer the casserole dish to the oven. After about 30 minutes the pork should have a beautiful roasted aroma and be just starting to soften up when you insert the tip of your knife. This dish is supposed to be rich and fatty, but you may want to tip off a little of the fat at this stage.

Cook the tomatoes in the oven at the same time as you are roasting the pork. Roast for about 20 minutes, or until the skins start to blister, then remove from the oven, pinch off the tomato skins and transfer the flesh to a bowl and squash them to a purée.

Lift the dish back onto the top of your stove over a medium heat and add the pancetta, garlic and shallots. Stir well and allow the pancetta and garlic to colour slightly, then add your clams and stir really well. Now add the puréed tomatoes and vermouth and cover with a lid until the clams have steamed open, which will take about 5 minutes. Take off the lid and add the chicken stock and thyme and gently simmer for a couple of moments. Taste your broth for seasoning and adjust if needed; when you are completely happy with everything, stir in your chopped parsley and take to the table with your fried potatoes on the side.

How to barbecue a whole fish

Now don't be scared, it is really quite simple. There are a few rules that should be followed and before you know it you'll be barbecuing a whole fish like a pro! Also, just to set your mind at ease, the first time you do it you may tear the skin or lose a tail — it's okay, don't stress, it happens to everyone.

Once you have a fish worthy of barbecuing and the barbecue itself, the rest is open to interpretation, but first a few details on the two key elements:

- The type of barbecue you use is completely up to you. The companies selling them will insist on the latest thing that does this and that — this will usually be made out of a beautiful piece of stainless steel and cost as much as your home. If you can, and feel inclined to do so, cook over coals that have formed from pieces of wood — the aroma is simply the best. But if you are not in the mood to build a fire an hour ahead of time to ensure a good bed of coals, then simply fire up the gas barbecue. Whichever method you use to produce the heat, just remember that when the fish actually goes on the barbecue you don't want too much heat. The heat should be hot but not screeching, and once the fish is on you need to maintain a good steady heat.
- Go to your fishmonger and buy yourself a beautiful, fresh, whole fish. That's about as specific as you should be about the species of fish you are to buy when you enter the shop. Why? Because your choice should always be driven by the markets, not by the recipe — if you are unsure what to buy, ask! One thing you need to keep in mind when buying whole fish is that you should only buy what you need, or be prepared to use the leftovers.

Okay, so the barbecue is hot (but not too hot), the fish is glistening, and it's time to put them together. Do as little as possible is my motto. Lightly score the fish if it is a thick, round fish, but don't bother if it's not. Lightly oil the fish, not the grill plate, and season really well with salt only (reserve the pepper for afterwards as I find it tends to scorch on the hot grill). Resist the urge to touch the fish once it hits the grill/hotplate. Let it sit there and allow the heat that comes directly to the fish from the grill to form a crust — this will ensure the fish doesn't stick. If you go to move the fish and it is stuck do not scrape it, just let it sit a little longer and eventually the fish will lift off.

Cook your fish almost two-thirds through on one side and then roll it over to cook the other side. Have everything else for the meal ready and on the table. Now, lift your fish onto a plate or platter, drizzle with a little extra virgin olive oil and season with a touch more salt and pepper and a dose of citrus in the form of lemon juice or lime juice.

Now that you have mastered the technique of buying and grilling beautiful fish, go crazy with possibilities of flavour, such as herbs, salts, flavoured salts, brushing snapper with beef dripping, stuffing salmon with wild fennel fronds … the possibilities are endless!

Roasted whole leatherjacket with romesco sauce

Serves 4

For the romesco sauce

6 large ripe tomatoes

1 bulb of garlic

60 ml (2 fl oz/¼ cup) olive oil for frying, plus extra, for drizzling

2 ancho chillies (a large dried chilli with a smoky flavour) or other large, dried chillies

500 ml (17 fl oz/2 cups) hot water

1 large stale croissant, thickly sliced

50 g (1¾ oz/⅓ cup) blanched almonds

50 g (1¾ oz/⅓ cup) hazelnuts, lightly toasted and skins removed

1 teaspoon paprika

60 ml (2 fl oz/¼ cup) red wine vinegar

salt and freshly ground black pepper

250 ml (9 fl oz/1 cup) extra virgin olive oil

You need to prepare a couple of the ingredients before you start to make the sauce base. Preheat your oven to 250°C (500°F/Gas 9). Take the tomatoes and cut them in half and place on a non-stick roasting tray, cut side down. Slice the bulb of garlic crossways, about two-thirds up the head, and place the larger half, cut side up, next to the tomatoes (reserve the remaining garlic). Drizzle with a little of the olive oil and place in the oven until the skin on the tomatoes starts to blister and the garlic gets nice and brown. You don't want any burnt bits but you do want a really good colour — this can take up to 30 minutes.

While the tomatoes and garlic are cooking, prepare the rest of the ingredients. Place a dry frying pan on a high heat, put the ancho chillies in the pan, press down with a spatula and scorch until you see a little wisp of smoke (about 10 seconds), then flip them over and scorch the other side. Remove from the pan and place into a bowl with the hot water and allow to soak for about 15 minutes, or until they soften. Remove the stem and any seeds, then set to one side.

Wipe out your frying pan and, while it is still hot, add the extra olive oil and gently fry the pieces of croissant for about 10 seconds on each side until golden brown, then drain on paper towel. Remove the remaining raw garlic from its skin and place into a food processor with the soaked chillies, nuts, paprika and the fried croissant. Blend really well, taking time to scrape down the side from time to time. By now your tomatoes should be ready, so take them out of the oven and, when cool enough to handle, pinch off the tomato skins and add the flesh and any cooking juices to the food processor. Take the garlic and squeeze out the roasted garlic flesh into the food processor bowl. Blend everything again with the vinegar and a good amount of salt and pepper. While the processor is running, very slowly add the extra virgin olive oil in a steady stream until everything is incorporated. Transfer the sauce to a bowl and taste, adding more salt, pepper and vinegar as required. This is now ready to use or you can store it in the fridge for up to 2 weeks.

For the roasted whole leatherjacket

4 x 300–400 g (10½ –14 oz) whole leatherjackets or other whole firm, white fish

300 ml (10½ fl oz) chicken or fish stock

a splash of dry white wine

vegetable oil, for frying

salt and freshly ground black pepper

For serving

2 tablespoons sesame seeds, toasted

a few sprigs of coriander (cilantro)

a few wedges of lime

Reduce the oven temperature to 200°C (400°F/Gas 6). Have your fishmonger clean the fish by removing the head (leatherjacket is one of the few fish I remove the head from before cooking) and cutting away the fins. If you are using another type of fish, leave the head on.

Start by pouring your stock and just a little white wine into a saucepan; when it has just come to the boil, add 500 g (1 lb 2 oz/2 cups) of your romesco sauce and give a really good stir. Place a lid on your saucepan and then turn the heat right down and let it barely simmer for about 30 minutes. The nuts and croissant in the romesco sauce will start to swell up and will give the sauce a nice consistency.

To cook the fish, either do it in batches in an ovenproof frying pan or roast them all together in one roasting tin. Start by heating the pan or roasting tin on the stove with a little oil; when the dish is very hot, season your fish and carefully add to your pan or tin. Cook on one side for about 5 minutes, then turn over and cook the other side for about 2 minutes until it is sealed. Tip off any excess oil and pour in your hot romesco sauce, then transfer the pan or tin to the oven and cook for about 8 minutes, or until the fish gives under your finger when you push it.

To serve, scatter the fish with toasted sesame seeds and coriander. Take the fish straight to the table and serve with wedges of lime. It goes well with a crisp salad.

Bass Grouper en papillote on carrot salad and piri piri

Serves 4

Buy your fish whole whenever you can, it is truly the best way to ensure quality and freshness. Filleting a fish is a very simple and very important skill for any cook to possess. It is also an absolutely crucial phase in the love and appreciation of a good-quality fish meal.

For the piri piri
1–2 small pieces of roasted capsicum (pepper), chopped
a good pinch of dried chilli flakes
200 ml (7 fl oz) extra virgin olive oil
80–100 ml (2½–3½ fl oz) lemon juice or white vinegar
salt, to taste

For the carrot salad
a good splash of olive oil
1 kg (2 lb 4 oz) carrots, baby carrots or dutch carrots, peeled and sliced lengthways if large
½ bunch rosemary, leaves picked
150 g (5½ oz) ginger, peeled and thinly sliced
3 large fresh red chillies, seeded and shredded
salt and freshly ground pepper

For the fish
1 egg white, lightly beaten
4 x 180–200 g (6¼–7 oz) bass grouper or other firm white fish, bones removed

To make the piri piri, put the capsicum and chilli flakes in a food processor or blender and blend to make a coarse purée. Add the olive oil, lemon juice and salt and blend just long enough to incorporate. Set aside.

To make the carrot salad, heat the olive oil in a large frying pan so that it is hot, but not smoking. Add your carrots and fry, tossing from time to time, to ensure you get a good, even colour. When they are close to being ready (test by inserting the tip of a knife into the carrots), add the rosemary, ginger and chilli and continue to cook, until the carrots are tender. Remove from the heat and allow to cool.

Preheat your oven to 190°C (375°F/Gas 5). Cut eight large 20 cm (8 inch) squares of baking paper.

To prepare the fish, take four of the squares and lightly brush the edges with a little egg white. Place a portion of the carrots in the middle of each paper square, then a piece of the fish, then a spoonful of the piri piri and season (use your judgement here, as you want to season the fish while taking into consideration the seasoning of the other ingredients). Place a square of baking paper over the top of each and turn and twist the paper together to seal the edges and enclose the fish.

Cook the fish parcels on a baking tray in the oven for about 14–16 minutes, then take the puffed-up paper parcels of aromatic steam and good times to the table to open in front of your guests.

Green

Greengrocer

Cured cucumbers

Serves 4

These cured cucumbers make a wonderfully crunchy, refreshing and invigorating snack. Three cheers for the easiest recipe in the book! This recipe is very loose — use one cucumber per person and adjust the quantities of the other ingredients to suit.

4 Lebanese (short) cucumbers
salt
sugar
lemon juice
finely chopped chives

Cut the cucumbers lengthways into quarters or sixths. Sprinkle the cut side with a little salt and sugar, then squeeze on a little lemon juice. Leave to sit like this in the fridge for a couple of hours. When you go to serve them remove from their liquid and sprinkle with a few finely chopped chives. They look particularly great standing up in an icy cold glass and placed next to a great big pitcher of Pimms!

Onion rings with parmesan mayo

Serves 4–6

This dish uses one of my favourite batter recipes. Although it is normally used in Indian cuisine and may seem a little out of context here, it works well. The parmesan mayo needs to be made from oil infused with parmesan rinds. If you don't have home-made parmesan oil, you can buy it from a gourmet food store, or make a plain mayonnaise instead.

For the chickpea flour batter

220 g (7¾ oz/2 cups) besan
  (chickpea flour)
175 g (6 oz/1 cup) rice flour
a pinch of asafoetida
a pinch of chilli powder
a pinch of salt
400 ml (14 fl oz) iced water in which
  1 teaspoon bicarbonate of soda
  (baking soda) has been dissolved

For the parmesan mayonnaise

juice of ½ lemon
2 egg yolks
a touch of dijon mustard
200 ml (7 fl oz) parmesan-infused oil
  (see page 197)
salt and freshly ground black pepper

For the onion rings

2 large onions
a touch of plain (all-purpose) flour
  for coating the onion rings
oil, for deep-frying
salt, to serve
wedges of lemon or lime, to serve

To make the chickpea flour batter, combine the dry ingredients in a large bowl, then make a well in the centre. Using a whisk, start to slowly add the iced water and gradually combine all of the ingredients into a batter that has the consistency of pouring cream. Keep in the fridge until you are ready to use it — the batter can be made the day before but don't try to keep it any longer than that.

To make the parmesan mayonnaise you can use a whisk, but it is easier in a food processor. Whisk or blend the lemon juice, egg yolks and mustard together. Slowly and carefully add your oil, making sure that it emulsifies before adding more. When you have finished adding your oil, season to taste with salt and pepper. Refrigerate until needed.

To make the onion rings, peel the onions, then cut into discs about 1 cm (½ inch) thick. Break the discs up into rings (the mystery of how this dish got its name is now revealed) and toss the rings in a little flour. Put the onion rings in the batter, shaking off any excess flour as you do so. When it comes to perfectly deep-frying the onion rings, read the introduction 'How to cook the perfect fries' (see pages 212–213). Take a large saucepan and fill it no more than one-third full of oil. Bring your oil up to 175°C (350°F), then carefully lower in a small batch of the onion rings and cook for 3–4 minutes, or until golden and crispy. Be careful not to overcook them as they really are at their best when crunchy on the outside and fluffy in the middle. Drain on paper towels. Repeat until all are cooked.

Serve the onion rings seasoned with a little salt with the parmesan mayonnaise on the side and some lemon and lime wedges for squeezing over.

Cauliflower and caper tapenade

Serves 10–12

I have a soft spot for cauliflower and I think I have my mum to thank for that. Mum was different from other mothers when I was a kid because she thought that cooking vegetables very briefly, until only just done meant they would retain goodness and flavour. All the other mothers I knew used to cook their vegetables to death and, unfortunately, cauliflower is the smelliest vegetable of them all when overcooked! I like this recipe because it utilises the sweet flavour and crunchy texture of cauliflower. Take this tapenade and serve it on anything from croutons to seared scallops.

200 g (7 oz) cauliflower, cut into florets
80 g (2¾ oz) salted capers, rinsed
60 g (2¼ oz) pitted green olives
a few sprigs of thyme, leaves only
1 small bunch of flat-leaf (Italian) parsley
¼ teaspoon finely grated lemon zest
150 ml (5 fl oz) extra virgin olive oil
salt and freshly ground black pepper

Blanch the cauliflower, then chop. Chop the capers, olives, thyme and parsley separately (chopping the thyme quite finely), then put all the chopped ingredients in a bowl with the lemon zest and oil. Mix well and taste for seasoning.

This tapenade will look fairly rustic. It is best served soon after being made, but it will keep quite well for 4–5 days in the fridge.

Asparagus with a warm coddled egg dressing

Serves 4

I like to serve this as a nice and easy starter and, when Mother Nature permits, I use green, white and purple asparagus. White asparagus is really the only one that I would ever be tempted to peel, as it tends to have slightly bitter skin. Purple asparagus loses a lot of colour as it cooks, but it does have a sweeter, milder flavour than green asparagus.

2 anchovy fillets
a pinch of chopped rosemary
60 ml (2 fl oz /¼ cup) pickled
  shallot vinegar (see page 234)
8 large eggs
80 ml (2½ fl oz /⅓ cup) extra virgin
  olive oil
salt and freshly ground black pepper
16 pieces of thick asparagus or
  enough for four people
a few sprigs of chervil, chopped

Let the asparagus tell you what to trim off; do this by taking hold of the bottom end and bending — it will break where it needs to. Never throw away your asparagus bottoms because they are perfectly good for soup. Or, to make asparagus stock, simply bring enough water to cover the asparagus to the boil, add your stems, boil for 10 minutes, then leave to infuse overnight in the fridge. Strain for a fragrant and green asparagus stock.

Have all of your ingredients ready because once you begin things will move pretty quickly and there will be no time for delays. You will need two pots of boiling salted water, one large enough for the eggs and the other large enough for the asparagus.

Using the back of a fork start crushing the anchovy fillets and rosemary with the vinegar in a small bowl. Put the eggs (in their shell) into one of the pots of boiling water and cook for 4 minutes. By this stage the whites should be just about cooked and only a little runny while the yolks will be completely runny.

Drain the eggs and hold the hot eggs with a cloth while you use a spoon to break them in half and scoop the egg whites and yolks into a bowl. Mash together lightly with a fork, leaving it slightly chunky. You must do this promptly, as you want your dressing to be served warm, and reheating is not really an option. Add the anchovy mixture, then slowly pour in the oil while mixing. Taste for seasoning.

Now, cook the asparagus in your second pot of boiling water — thick asparagus will need about 6 minutes, thinner less time. It is always a good idea to test the asparagus after a couple of minutes, this will give you an idea of how quickly it is cooking. One thing about asparagus — you want it to have a firm texture, but it should not have a 'crunch' to it. Asparagus that is undercooked has a slightly acidic flavour.

Once cooked, drain well and arrange on a platter, then add the chopped chervil to the dressing and pour over the top of the asparagus. Serve immediately.

Olives roasted with rosemary and orange

Makes 1.5 litres (52 fl oz/6 cups)

You've got to love this recipe. Make it when you have a couple of moments to spare and keep the olives in a jar in the fridge until you want them. They taste great and look awesome and are as versatile as any olive. I like to keep the oil even after the olives have been eaten and use it to make dressings or to pour over bruschetta. Like many of my recipes, use the quantities given as a guide. I am more interested in opening you up to opportunities than dictating to you how much rosemary or garlic you should like to eat!

1 kg (2 lb 4 oz) manzanilla olives in brine (you can use kalamata olives, ligurian olives or whatever takes your fancy but don't use pitted olives)

1 bulb of garlic, broken into cloves, with the skins left on

3 stalks of rosemary

a generous pinch of freshly ground black pepper

about 500 ml (17 fl oz/2 cups) extra virgin olive oil

the peel and juice of 2 oranges, peel cut into strips

Start by rinsing the brine off your olives. Put the rinsed olives in a large saucepan with the cloves of garlic, rosemary stalks, pepper, oil and orange peel. Bring up to a very gentle simmer and cook for about 10 minutes. Add the orange juice and cook for another 15 minutes or so until you have soft cloves of garlic and olives that are just starting to wrinkle. The cooking time will vary slightly depending on the type and size of your olives — large kalamata olives will take slightly longer, tiny ligurian olives will take no time at all.

Cool slightly, then transfer everything to a 1.5 litre (52 fl oz/6-cup) sterilised jar: it is always advisable to use sterilised containers when storing food. If stored correctly (in a sterilised jar out of direct sunlight, preferably in the fridge) these olives should last for months. The oil will solidify, but this is okay as it will liquefy when brought to room temperature.

Chive tarts with enoki mushroom salad

Makes 50

This is a great recipe that is easily adapted to suit just about any soft herb, and then you get to change the toppings. For instance, you could try chervil tarts with a small dollop of sour cream, or parsley tarts with salmon roe. I have made the assumption that you don't want to spend too much time on these so I am using pre-baked tartlet cases.

For the chive tarts

50 x 3 cm (1¼ inch) ready-made tartlet shells
2 bunches of chives, finely chopped
185 ml (6 fl oz/¾ cup) milk (full-cream/whole milk gives the best results; skim milk tends to foam too much during the blending process)
1 whole egg and 2 egg yolks, lightly beaten together
30 ml (1 fl oz) pouring (whipping) cream
½ teaspoon dijon mustard
salt and freshly ground black pepper

For the enoki mushroom salad

200 g (7 oz) enoki mushrooms
1 tablespoon truffle oil or good-quality extra virgin olive oil
2 tablespoons freshly grated parmesan cheese
a dash of lemon juice
a sprinkle of chopped chives
salt and freshly ground black pepper

Preheat your oven to 120°C (235°F/Gas ½). Lay out the tartlet shells on baking trays. You get the best results for the custard if you have a good-quality, high-speed upright blender that will allow you to completely pulverise the chives. Put the chives and milk into your blender or food processor and purée. Don't let the mixture blend for too long as you do not want to heat or curdle the milk.

If you feel you have to strain the mixture do so into a bowl, being sure to squeeze as much as you can from the chives, otherwise just throw it all in. Use a spatula or wooden spoon to add the egg, cream and mustard to the chive milk. You don't want to mix too much or you will aerate your custard — mix until well combined, no more. The easiest thing to do now is to transfer your mixture into a pitcher or bowl with a spout, and from there pour it into your tartlet shells.

Bake for about 8–12 minutes. What you are looking for is a 'just set' custard. One test is to tap the edge of a tart shell with your finger — it is ready if the custard doesn't wobble twice. If the tarts require longer, then check them often as they will cook fairly quickly because they are so small. If the custard starts to rise, they need to come out of the oven promptly — don't despair, they will still be lovely to eat. Allow to cool completely, but don't refrigerate.

To make the enoki mushroom salad, slice the mushrooms into 5 mm (¼ inch) pieces, cutting as far as the stems are separated — discard the 'clump' at the bottom. Gently toss all of the ingredients in a bowl and season.

Just before you are ready to serve, place small tidy mounds of the enoki mushroom salad on top of each cool tart, using all the salad. Serve immediately.

Pickled coleslaw

Serves 8

In my part of the world coleslaw conjures images of limp cabbage in a watery, gloopy mayonnaise on an all-you-can-eat buffet. But Michael Klausen, a very dear friend and an inspirational cook, showed me this recipe and changed my world for the better even though I don't like eating cabbage as a salad and can't abide the flavour of green capsicum. I make this at home often, and crave it when I don't have any made in the fridge. It goes really well with ham, pork and roast chicken.

1 litre (35 fl oz /4 cups) cider vinegar
800 g (1 lb 12 oz /3⅔ cups) sugar
1 tablespoon celery seeds
1 onion, finely diced
2 green capsicums (peppers), finely diced
800 ml (28 fl oz) water
1 large white cabbage, shredded
salt and freshly ground black pepper

To make the brine, pour the vinegar into a large saucepan and add the sugar, celery seeds, onion and capsicum. Bring to the boil for 15 minutes then add the water.

You will need a non-metallic container large enough to hold all of the ingredients. Start by scattering a layer of cabbage, salt and pepper in the base of the container and spoon on some of the brine. Then add some more cabbage, salt, pepper and brine. Keep going until everything is used — you will probably have to really push the cabbage down towards the end. You want to place a weight on top of the cabbage to make sure that it stays immersed; I normally use a dinner plate or tray.

Cover and allow everything to pickle for at least 24 hours at room temperature or 48 hours in the fridge. This will keep perfectly fine in your cupboard for a couple of weeks; it will last indefinitely in your fridge.

Radicchio di treviso with fried onions, parmesan and balsamic

Serves 4

For simple meals like this salad, it's important to use great ingredients. So, with that in mind, use as good an extra virgin olive oil and balsamic vinegar as you can. Ideally you're looking for a thick, peppery olive oil and an aged vinegar — trust me, the flavour will be well worth the expense. Also, don't use anything other than a mature parmesan cheese.

2 red onions
1 teaspoon salt
1 teaspoon sugar
vegetable oil, for deep-frying
4 heads of radicchio di treviso
100 ml (3½ fl oz) thick, peppery extra virgin olive oil
80 ml (2½ fl oz/⅓ cup) aged balsamic vinegar
1 bunch of flat-leaf (Italian) parsley, coarsely chopped
freshly ground black pepper
a block of mature parmesan cheese

When you've finished with the block of parmesan cheese, keep the rinds to use in the ribollita recipe on pages 286–287. To store them, put them in a jar and cover with olive oil. You'll find that you'll not only preserve your rinds this way, but you will end up with a delicious parmesan-infused oil that you can use in salad dressings and also for the parmesan mayonnaise on page 188.

Thinly slice the onions, then put them in a bowl. Season with the salt and sugar, toss together, then let it sit like this for a couple of hours. Squeeze out as much liquid from the onion as you can.

You'll need a heavy-based saucepan for the next step. Heat enough vegetable oil in the pan to deep-fry the onions, but don't overfill the pan because you are working with hot oil. As a general rule, only fill your pan one-third or one-half full of oil when deep-frying. Put the onion in the oil as it is warming up — don't wait for the oil to become hot. Cook the onion over high heat, stirring often, making sure to keep an eye on it as it will do nothing for ages and then colour quickly towards the end. When it becomes a pale golden colour (it will continue to colour after you have removed it from the oil) work quickly and carefully to remove it with a slotted spoon and drain on crumpled paper towels. Gently toss the onion a couple of times to ensure the pieces don't clump together. When the onion is completely cool taste it for seasoning and add more salt or sugar accordingly.

Take the radicchio and remove and discard the thicker outside leaves, then cut in half lengthways, shred finely and put in a large bowl, trying to keep it all together and tidy. If it comes apart it doesn't matter too much. Drizzle on your olive oil, splash in your vinegar and sprinkle on the onion and parsley. Grind in some black pepper and, using a vegetable peeler, shave in a generous amount of parmesan. Instead of tossing your salad, gently 'roll' it with your hands, this will incorporate all of the ingredients but will keep it tidy. Taste your salad and make adjustments where needed. To serve, grab a 'bundle' of the finished salad and place it next to a wedge of good bread. Shave a little more parmesan over the top to finish.

Asian green salad with nahm jhim

Serves 4

While Asian greens are not usually considered a 'salad green' this dish is big on flavour, with a good touch of heat from the chillies and a slightly pickled character. The trick to this dish, as with any of my recipes, is to use the best produce of the day. You can substitute any vegetable here for another — what makes the salad special is that you make a powerful Vietnamese-style dressing, known as nahm jim, to enhance wonderful vegetables that have been cooked to perfection. You can adjust the heat of the dressing by altering the number of chillies and whether you include the seeds or not (the more seeds, the hotter the dressing).

For the nahm jim

2–3 bird's eye chillies

3 French shallots

1 clove of garlic

roots from 1 bunch of coriander (cilantro) (you'll need the leaves for the salad)

85 g (3 oz) palm sugar (jaggery), shaved

80 ml (2½ fl oz/⅓ cup) lime juice

80 ml (2½ fl oz/⅓ cup) fish sauce

For the toasted rice

100 g (3½ oz/½ cup) jasmine rice

To make the nahm jim, you need either a very large mortar and pestle or a small food processor. A mortar and pestle will give the best results because pounding all of your ingredients into a fine paste helps to release the flavour, giving a nicer texture to the dressing. Cut your chillies in half — whether or not you remove the seeds is up to you.

Place the chillies, shallots, garlic and coriander roots in the mortar or food processor and pound or blend really well — be careful that the chilli does not splash out and get you in the eyes. When your solid ingredients become a paste, add the palm sugar and pound or process until dissolved, then, using a stirring motion, add the lime juice and fish sauce. Your dressing should be very intense but have a good balance of heat (chilli), salt (fish sauce), sweet (palm sugar) and sour (lime juice). After you taste your dressing you may need to adjust the seasoning accordingly until it is balanced. Set aside.

To make the toasted rice, put the rice in a clean, dry, cold frying pan and toast over low heat until the rice is a pale straw colour. Allow it to cool, then grind with your mortar and pestle until you have a fine powder. Set aside.

For the vegetables
½ Chinese cabbage (wong bok)
1 bunch of bok choy (pak choy)
1 bunch of choy sum (Chinese
  flowering cabbage)
1 bunch of gai larn (Chinese broccoli)
a pinch of salt

For serving
1 bunch of mint, leaves picked
the leaves from the bunch of
  coriander (cilantro) left from the
  nahm jim
a small knob of ginger (young ginger
  if available), peeled and cut into
  thin strips

To prepare your vegetables, you first need to make a decision about what size to cut them; this will depend a lot on their natural size. What you are aiming for is all the chopped vegetables to be roughly the same size, but the size you pick is up to you. When in doubt, 3–4 cm (1¼–1½ inch) pieces usually work well. It's worthwhile keeping in mind that if your pieces are too large the dish will be tricky to serve.

Cook the vegetables briefly in plenty of well-seasoned boiling water, then plunge into iced water and, finally, drain off all the excess water (too much water on your greens means you will end up diluting your dressing). The cooking time depends on your vegetable: the cabbage needs no more than 30 seconds and the vegetables with thick stalks can take 2–4 minutes, but their leaves need less time. Start tasting your vegetables after they have been plunged into boiling water and remove them when you judge them to be perfect.

To serve, simply ensure your vegetables are dry, and combine them in a large bowl with your mint and coriander leaves, ginger strips and add most of your dressing (reserve a little to finish the salad). Toss well and taste, adding more dressing or nahm jim ingredients as required; for example, if you think it needs to taste sourer, add an extra squeeze of lime. When you are completely happy with the flavour, mound your salad onto a platter, splash over a little more dressing and sprinkle with the toasted rice.

Hasselback potatoes with L'edel de cleron and a hazelnut dressing

Serves 6

If you like a roasted potato, then the hasselback is a guaranteed winner! The way the potato is sliced gives it a wonderful texture with a satisfying crunch on the outside, and it allows all of the cheese and dressing to fall into the fluffy flesh of the potato. As for how many potatoes to cook, I would allow at least three per person, but don't cook too many more unless you want to serve them on their own as they are quite rich. I like to use small cocktail potatoes for this as they make perfect one-bite mouthfuls.

For the toasted hazelnut dressing
100 g (3½ oz/¾ cup) hazelnuts
½ clove of garlic
60 ml (2 fl oz/¼ cup) extra virgin olive oil
½ lemon, zest cut into strips, juiced
salt and freshly ground black pepper
small pinch of sugar

Preheat your oven to 120°C (235°F/Gas ½). To make the toasted hazelnut dressing, lay the hazelnuts onto a baking tray and lightly bake for 10–12 minutes, or just until you see the skins start to split and the nut take on a little colour. One thing to know about toasting hazelnuts is that they will take more colour in the centre of the nut than on the outside, so if you are cooking by eye (that is, looking at the colour of the nut) you should always cook them a little less than you would for other nuts. When you are happy with the nuts, tip them out onto a dry tea towel (dish towel) and wrap them; let them sit like this for a moment and then gently rub to loosen all of the skins from the nut — if a few little shards of skin remain attached to the nut, this is fine.

Carefully remove the hazelnuts from the tea towel and place them onto a chopping board. Use the flat of a knife to crack the hazelnuts into rough pieces; while you are doing this, take your garlic and squash it with the flat of your knife but leave in one piece.

Place the hazelnuts into a frying pan with the garlic, olive oil and 3 or 4 strips of lemon. Place your pan onto a high heat and cook for about 4–5 minutes. When you are happy with the beautiful golden colour on the nuts and garlic and the room has a delicious warming hazelnut aroma, remove your pan from the heat and add the juice from your lemon. Taste for seasoning, adding more lemon juice if required, then adding salt, pepper and sugar — the aim is for a well-balanced vinaigrette. Set aside at room temperature.

For the potatoes

3–4 potatoes per person, such as
  chat or nicola
butter, at room temperature
salt and freshly ground black pepper

For serving

1 wheel L'edel de cleron or other
  beautiful Vacherin-style cheese
salt and freshly ground black pepper

L'edel de cleron is a soft, ripened Vacherin-style cheese with a white mould rind. When ripe, it is rich and flavoursome while at the same time staying fairly delicate, but a brie or camembert would also work well here. One thing that many people do not understand is that cheese, like any good produce, ripens as it ages and has a peak period when it is at its best. Depending on the type of cheese, once it reaches this point it will last for a couple of days or a couple of months.

Preheat your oven to 220°C (425°F/Gas 7). To cook the potatoes, slice off a little from the bottom of the potato so they can stand up without wobbling — look at your potatoes to see if there is a slight mark and make that the bottom.

Now comes the fiddly bit. The best knife to use to 'hasselback' the potatoes is one that is sharp and thin. Place the potato on your chopping board, cut side down. Starting at one end, slice the potato almost all the way down but not through the base. Make parallel cuts 1 mm ($\frac{1}{32}$ inch) apart all the way along the potato. Repeat with the rest of the potatoes. Place your potatoes on a greased baking tray and rub each potato with plenty of butter, then season with salt and pepper.

Place the potatoes into the oven and roast for about 30 minutes; halfway through the cooking process, brush the potatoes with a little more butter. The potatoes are cooked when you have a nice golden crust and they are tender in the centre when tested with a knife.

To serve, place the potatoes on a platter while they are still hot and spoon a generous amount of the cheese over them. Drizzle with some of the hazelnut dressing, being sure to mound some of the nuts on top. Season with a little more salt and pepper and serve as soon as possible.

Fennel & celeriac served with toasted almond & bacon fat dressing

Serves 8

The idea of cooking in fat might not be to everyone's liking, but it does taste delicious. The reason I like to use back fat here is that it gives an almost creamy finish to the dressing, and the bold clean flavours of the root vegetables respond really well to this. If you have trouble getting hold of pork back fat you can substitute duck fat.

1 large head of celeriac
  (about 500 g/1 lb 2 oz), cut into
  8 wedges
1 star anise
salt and freshly ground black pepper
2 large heads of fennel, cut into
  quarters
a knob of butter
250 g (9 oz) piece of pork back fat,
  diced fairly small
100 g (3½ oz/⅔ cup) blanched
  almonds, roughly broken with the
  flat of your knife
1 clove of garlic, crushed
a little chopped thyme and chopped
  flat-leaf (Italian) parsley
a splash of white wine vinegar

Preheat your oven to 120°C (235°F/Gas ½). Put the celeriac wedges in a saucepan and cover with cold water. Add the star anise, salt and black pepper and bring to a gentle simmer. Now add your fennel. Cook the vegetables for about 8–10 minutes, or until tender, then drain and gently toss with a knob of butter and a little more ground black pepper. Transfer the vegetables to a large casserole dish and put into a warm oven.

To make the dressing, put the diced fat in a small frying pan and start to fry over a medium heat, stirring from time to time. You will not need to add any oil as the fat will start to render. When the edges just start to brown, add the almonds, turn the heat up to high and fry everything together until well browned. When you have a delicious nutty aroma and a good brown colour, remove your pan from the heat and add the garlic clove and leave to cook in the heat of the pan. After a moment, add your herbs, vinegar and salt and pepper to taste — you want a good balance of sharpness for a well-flavoured dressing.

Remove your vegetables from the oven (they should have dried slightly by now), scoop into serving dishes and spoon the dressing over the top.

Slow-cooked broccoli and bitter greens pie

Serves 6–8

Before you even think about starting this recipe, you need to put to one side all common thinking about cooking broccoli. You need to get your head around the fact that you will not be cooking the broccoli briefly in order to keep it bright and crunchy — instead you will be cooking your broccoli slowly until it becomes quite soft. Now before you go rolling your eyes skyward and thinking I have gone crazy, slow-cooked broccoli does not mean overcooked broccoli. What it does mean is that you will be cooking your vegetable until it transforms into something quite brilliant. It has a really rich, warm and nutty flavour that lends itself to an old-fashioned hearty pie. I have paired the broccoli with a couple of other greens here but you can easily substitute any of these for something else; I often use turnip tops or beetroot (beet) tops.

For the olive oil pastry
280 g (10 oz/2¼ cups) plain
  (all-purpose) flour
½ teaspoon salt
1½ tablespoons olive oil
135 ml (4½ fl oz) water

To make the pastry, combine the flour and salt in a large bowl and make a well in the centre, then add the olive oil and water and form into a firm dough, adding a little more water if it is too dry. Wrap your dough up really well in a piece of plastic wrap and let this rest for at least 2 hours in the fridge, then keep at room temperature for a few minutes before rolling the pastry. Resting the dough makes it a lot easier to work with — if you try rolling the dough straight away, you will find it rubbery and hard to work with.

Grease a 28 cm (11¼ inch) pie tin. Roll out the pastry until it is large enough to fit into your tin, with a little hanging over the edges, and allow this to rest for another 30 minutes. Trim any overhanging excess pastry before filling.

For the filling

1 large head of broccoli (about
  400 g/14 oz)

2 onions, finely diced

125 ml (4 fl oz/½ cup) olive oil

2 large red chillies, split and seeded

salt and freshly ground black pepper

100 ml (3½ fl oz) dry white wine

1 large bunch of rapini (broccoli
  raab) or silverbeet (Swiss chard)

2 potatoes, boiled in their skins,
  peeled and diced into 1 cm
  (½ inch) cubes

1 large handful of rocket (arugula),
  coarsely chopped

1 large handful of flat-leaf (Italian)
  parsley, chopped

a touch of fresh marjoram

4 eggs, lightly beaten together

For the pie

200 g (7 oz) feta cheese, crumbled

To make the filling, trim only the very bottom of the broccoli stem, leaving on as much of the stem as possible, then use a vegetable peeler to remove the fibrous thick green skin from the lower portion of the broccoli stem. Cut the broccoli lengthways into about eight evenly sized wedges.

In a large saucepan, combine the onion and about half of the olive oil and cook over a low heat until the onion is nice and soft, but does not colour. Add the chilli and broccoli, season well with salt and pepper and splash in the white wine. Cover your pan and cook over a very low heat for 30 minutes, stirring very gently from time to time. The broccoli is ready when it is completely soft. Preheat your oven to 190°C (375°F/Gas 5).

While the broccoli is cooking, wilt the other greens. If you are using rapini, then simply cut the leafy ends into 2–3 cm (¾–1¼ inch) pieces; if you are using silverbeet, remove the white stem and chop the leaves. You will need to wilt the greens in batches; do this by placing some of your leaves into a large flat pan with a drizzle of the olive oil and a little water, gently cook until they have become nice and soft, then transfer to a bowl to cool. When all of the leaves are cooked and cooled, use your hands to squeeze out as much of the liquid as possible, then place into a clean bowl with the potato, rocket, herbs and eggs. When the broccoli is cooked, gently lift it out and set aside; mix the onion and cooking juices into the greens and potato mixture.

Place all of the filling into the pastry case — your broccoli will mush up a little but that is okay, just try to be gentle so you get as much in one piece as possible. Crumble the feta over the top, then bake the pie for about 45 minutes.

Carrot and coriander seed salad

Serves 4–6

This is an incredibly easy salad to prepare. All the ingredients are there to enhance the natural flavour of the carrot, so you need to have the best possible carrots: juicy, sweet and flavoursome. The type, size and shape of the carrot are secondary to the flavour, so make sure you taste a little piece of carrot before going any further.

500 g (1 lb 2 oz) carrots
a pinch of salt
a pinch of sugar
2½ tablespoons coriander seeds, lightly toasted, then roughly crushed
1 small stalk of rosemary, leaves picked
1–2 large red chillies, seeded and thinly sliced lengthways
60 ml (2 fl oz/¼ cup) verjuice or mild white wine vinegar
80 ml (2½ fl oz/⅓ cup) extra virgin olive oil
salt and freshly ground black pepper

Start by preparing your carrots, which for this recipe means doing as little as possible to them. If you are using baby carrots, perhaps just gently scrape off the skin and leave them whole; if you are using great big carrots, then they may need to be peeled and cut into pieces — the decision is up to you.

Bring a saucepan of water to a rolling boil and add a good pinch of salt and the same amount of sugar, then add the carrots and cook them for the briefest time possible — they must still be wonderfully sweet and crunchy. When they are cooked to your liking, lift them out of the water and plunge into iced water to stop the cooking process. As soon as they are cool, drain, then put them in a large bowl.

In a separate bowl, add the coriander seeds, rosemary, chilli, verjuice and olive oil and gently whisk to combine the flavours. Add some salt and ground black pepper and taste again. Pour the dressing over the carrots and toss them together really well, then let them sit for at least an hour. Taste them again before serving to see if you need to alter the seasoning, as the chilli will have started to come out and the verjuice will have penetrated the carrots.

Celeriac and port soup

Serves 6

I loooove celeriac — it's a lumpy, warty-looking beast with a sweet, aromatic delicious flesh — beauty in the beast!

1 small onion, sliced
a knob of butter
salt and freshly ground black pepper
1 small all-purpose potato (such as desiree), peeled and sliced
800 g–1 kg (1 lb 12 oz–2 lb 4 oz) celeriac, peeled and thinly sliced
1 litre (35 fl oz/4 cups) milk
a dash of pouring (whipping) cream
300 ml (10½ fl oz) port

You need a heavy-based saucepan with a tight-fitting lid to make this soup. Put the onion and butter in the pan and add a little salt. Put on the lid and sit the pan over a low heat, stirring from time to time to prevent sticking, but keep the lid on as much as possible — you are trying to extract the sweet juices from the onion. Once the onion is soft, add the potato and celeriac, then replace the lid and keep the heat low — you are trying to soften the root vegetables before adding the liquid. Keep an eye on the vegetables as the potato and celeriac will stick easily. When the vegetables are just starting to become tender, about 15 minutes, add the milk and cook without the lid for another 20 minutes or so until everything has become soft. Allow to cool slightly before blending. Using a blender, purée your soup and pass it through a fine sieve. Add a dash of cream and taste for seasoning

While your soup is cooking reduce the port to a syrup that looks like honey. To do this pour the port into a small saucepan and place over a high heat. Keep the port on a rapid boil until it has reduced by about two-thirds. If the alcohol catches on fire, don't panic, it will only burn for a moment and will go out by itself.

To serve this soup I like to leave the celeriac soup smooth and white and ladle this into bowls, then add a drizzle of the port reduction over the top.

How to cook the perfect fries

To cook perfect fries you will need all of the normal utensils, such as a large heavy-based saucepan, a slotted spoon or 'spider' to lift the fries out of the oil and a tray with plenty of paper for draining the fries. Another important piece of equipment is a thermometer (it needs to be a candy or deep-frying thermometer) as it is the most accurate way to test the oil, but if you don't have one I will give you a tip. If you take a small cube of plain bread and drop it into oil that is 175°C (350°F) it will take about 45 seconds for it to go golden brown.

About the potato. A large baking potato such as sebago is my favourite; you can get away with a good all-rounder potato, such as desiree, but avoid anything too waxy or wet, such as kipfler (fingerling) or nicola. You want to cut your fry no thicker than 1 cm (½ inch). If you are doing a large quantity put the cut fries in water to stop them from discolouring, but if you are only doing a small batch, then cut them as you place them into the oil for the first frying.

About the oil. I prefer the neutral flavour of cottonseed oil or vegetable oil but beef dripping or duck fat make a wonderful substitute for those who enjoy a more robust flavour. The oil needs to have a high enough smoking point for you to be able to cook without it smoking and giving off an acrid flavour — extra virgin olive oil, for example, is not a good choice as it will start to smoke at a low temperature and its flavour will overpower the potato. The oil will be used twice — one of the secrets to great fries is that you need to cook the potato twice.

About the salt. When you eat a fry, you are eating potato and salt and that's about it. Sounds pretty obvious but it often gets overlooked. So this might be a good time to give you a lesson about salt. First of all, salt is salt. All salt has exactly the same chemical make up — what distinguishes the different types is how and where the salt was refined. The shape and size of salt are important and it's important to know the different options so you choose the right type to match the food you are seasoning. Try the following experiment. Take three pieces of a raw vegetable, such as a tomato or celery. Using about the same quantity of salt, season the first with normal fine ground table salt, the second with a few lumps of rock salt and the third with salt flakes. When you eat the vegetables you will notice that the table salt will taste immediately saltier as the salt easily dissolves straight away and your taste buds get a big salt hit all in one go. Now try the large rock salt — you will get the flavour of unsalted vegetable and then little salt bursts, which give a 'tasty' effect. The salt flakes tend to be a good compromise as they will dissolve slightly as you eat. But when it comes to fries, you'll find that if you use large rock salt or even salt flakes, the salt will simply fall off and do nothing to the potato. So, in short, salt flakes have a nice aesthetic quality but to season your fries correctly you should use a fine powdered table salt.

For the fries

oil, for deep-frying

about 1 large potato per person

table salt or celeriac salt (see below), for sprinkling

Take a large saucepan and fill it no higher than one-third full of oil. Using a large chopping knife, cut your potatoes no thicker than 1 cm (½ inch) and soak them in cold water. This will keep them from browning and will rinse off some of the starch. Remove your potatoes from the water and pat dry — this is very important as you do not want to throw water into your pan of hot oil.

Heat your oil to 140°C (275°F) and start to blanch your fries. Do not overcrowd your pan as you will make the temperature of the oil drop and your fries will not cook correctly. After 3 minutes of cooking, carefully lift out your fries and drain on paper towel. This stage can be done in advance, in fact even 1 day before; of course they are better when you cook them straight away.

When you are ready to serve your fries, bring your oil up to 175°C (350°F) and carefully lower in your fries in batches and cook for 3–4 minutes, or until golden and crispy. Be careful not to overcook the fries as they really are at their best when crunchy on the outside and fluffy in the middle. Drain on paper towel and sprinkle with salt.

To make celeriac salt you can peel and grate 1 head of celeriac and combine on a tray with an equal amount of salt (for example, 1 cup salt to 1 cup celeriac). Mix together well, then leave this to dry completely by sitting in the sun out of the wind or by placing in an oven on its lowest possible temperature and stirring from time to time to ensure it dries out properly. When the mixture is dry, use a mortar and pestle to ground to a powder and store in an airtight container for up to 2 months.

Celeriac and celery salad

Serves 4

This is a great salad using beautiful raw autumnal vegetables. It's hearty enough to serve on its own as a lunch dish. The salsa verde will make more than you need and will keep for at least 2 weeks in the fridge — try it on grilled meat.

For the celery salsa verde

1 head of celery

½ bunch of flat-leaf (Italian) parsley

1 clove of garlic

8 anchovy fillets

120 g (4¼ oz/¾ cup) salted capers, soaked for 2 hours, then rinsed and squeezed dry

extra virgin olive oil

salt and freshly ground black pepper

For serving

1 head of celeriac

1 lemon

a pinch of salt

about 100 g (3½ oz) piece of young pecorino cheese (it needs to be soft enough to crumble)

4 soft-boiled eggs, peeled

To make the celery salsa verde, remove all of the celery leaves from the celery. Now the chopping begins — you can do this in the food processor but you will get a much better result if you use a sharp chopping knife. Finely chop the following: 2 stalks of celery, the celery leaves, parsley, garlic, anchovies and capers. Combine all of your ingredients in a bowl and stir in enough extra virgin olive oil to form a paste. Taste your salsa verde and adjust the seasoning accordingly but just keep in mind that the salt from the capers and anchovies will develop more as it sits so don't add too much salt.

To assemble the salad, peel your celeriac and slice about 2 mm (¹⁄₁₆ inch) thick, then carefully cut the slices into thin batons, but not too thin. Place the celeriac in a bowl, squeeze over the lemon juice and sprinkle with salt and combine really well, then let this sit for a couple of minutes. Now add half your salsa verde and combine really well. Present the salad on a platter and, to finish, crumble over your pecorino cheese and break your soft boiled eggs over the top.

As an alternative, this salad can be served warm if you wish — simply blanch the celeriac in boiling salted water for no more than 10–15 seconds so the pieces still retain their crunch and then dress in the salsa verde.

Watermelon and fennel salad

Serves 6

I still remember the first time I ate watermelon as a kid. It was a hot day at the beach and my mum pulled out a huge red wedge of fruit from the cool box. I buried my face in the cool juicy melon and was immediately in heaven! This recipe is another example of the many uses of the humble watermelon.

1 small, deliciously sweet and juicy watermelon, rind removed and diced into 2 cm (¾ inch) cubes
2 heads of fennel, trimmed and finely diced
1 tablespoon fennel seeds, lightly toasted
extra virgin olive oil
a squeeze of lemon juice (optional)
wild fennel salt (see below) or salt and freshly ground black pepper

Place the watermelon and fennel in a large bowl and toss well to combine.

Crush the fennel seeds using a mortar and pestle and add a little olive oil and lemon juice to the mortar to form a nice smooth dressing. Pour over the watermelon and fennel, season with the wild fennel salt, or salt and pepper, and toss gently to combine.

Wild fennel salt is easily made by combining wild fennel fronds with sea salt and leaving them for 2–3 days until the fennel has completely dried. The dried fronds are then ground using a mortar and pestle. Wild fennel can be found beside rivers, some parks and the occasional abandoned construction site or neglected garden.

Pea and lettuce risotto

Serves 6–8

A little note to the first-time risotto cooker. Risotto should be soft and silky in texture, with a good amount of butter and cheese. The amount you actually add is going to rely on your own preference (I like loads of both), but you really do not need to be heavy-handed. Remember, it is easier to add more butter and cheese at the end than to take it out.

For the pea stock
800 g (1 lb 2 oz) fresh peas
some soft herb stalks

For the pea juice
2 kg (4 lb 8 oz) peas

For the chive oil
1 bunch chives, finely chopped
80 ml (2½ fl oz/⅓ cup) vegetable oil

For the risotto
200 g (7 oz) butter, chopped
2 celery stalks, finely diced
2 garlic cloves, crushed
360 g (12¾ oz/1⅔ cups) arborio rice
1 iceberg lettuce, very finely shredded
1 litre (35 fl oz/4 cups) sugar snap pea juice (see recipe below)
50 g (1¾ oz) grana padano cheese, grated
500 g (1 lb 2 oz) golden enoki mushrooms, steamed, to serve

Pod all of the peas and place the pea shells in the saucepan, reserving the peas for the risotto. Add the herb stalks and enough water so that the peas are not quite covered. Bring to simmer and cook for 5 minutes. Remove from the heat and transfer to a food processor or use a stick blender to make a chunky purée. Strain the pea stock through a fine sieve and use or refrigerate immediately.

To make the pea juice, put the sugar snap peas in a juicer and extract the juice. Set aside.

To make the chive oil, put the chives and vegetable oil in a food processor or blender and process until well combined and smooth. Pass through a fine sieve and use as directed. Chive oil can be stored in the fridge for 1 day.

To make the risotto, bring the pea stock to a simmer. Heat 60 g (2¼ oz) of the butter in a large heavy-based saucepan over medium heat. Add the celery and garlic and cook until just starting to soften. Add the rice and cook, stirring continuously. Gradually add the hot pea stock, a ladleful at a time, stirring constantly so the stock is absorbed before adding more. Continue until all of the stock is used the rice is cooked. Pour the rice out onto a tray in a single layer and set aside to cool.

Cook the freshly podded peas in a large saucepan of boiling water. Drain and place the peas in a saucepan, then add the cooled rice and stir well to combine. Add the lettuce and enough of the sugar snap pea juice to ensure the risotto is moist, soft and a vibrant green colour. Cook over medium heat until the lettuce has softened, add some of the remaining chopped butter and the parmesan, tasting as you go and stirring until creamy and soft.

Stir in the chives, then divide between serving plates, drizzle with the chive oil and serve with the enoki mushrooms on top, if desired.

Pasta stuffed with roasted pumpkin with ox-heart tomato & pecorino cheese

Serves 6

This is a really fun-looking dish, hearty and bold. One thing to keep in mind here is that when you go to finish your pasta in the ox-heart tomato mixture you may think the sauce doesn't look quite right. But what happens is that the tomato will break down as the pasta heats up. The end result is a juicy looking pasta sauce that isn't too wet.

For the roasted pumpkin filling

1 small butternut pumpkin (squash), peeled and cut into large dice
2 cloves of garlic, sliced
a large pinch of chilli flakes
1 stalk of rosemary, leaves only
salt and freshly ground black pepper
a good dash of extra virgin olive oil

For the filled pasta shells

400 g (14 oz) lumaconi (or large macaroni, rigatoni or conchiglioni)
a dash of extra virgin olive oil

Preheat your oven to 200°C (400°F/Gas 6). To make the roasted pumpkin filling, heat a roasting tin in the oven to get it nice and hot. Combine the pumpkin, garlic, chilli flakes, rosemary leaves and salt and pepper in a bowl with a good dash of extra virgin olive oil. Tip the pumpkin into the roasting tin, then put into the hot oven. You want to get a golden roasted colour on your pumpkin and to cook it until it is soft — this will take about 20 minutes. Allow the pumpkin mix to cool slightly, then transfer to a bowl and use a wooden spoon to mash the mixture until a coarse purée forms.

To fill make the pasta shells, boil the pasta in plenty of salted water for about 8 minutes, or until al dente. Strain it into a colander and give it a little shake, being sure to get off as much water as possible. Tip the pasta onto a tray, drizzle with a little oil and give a very gentle toss to lightly coat the pasta. Allow it to cool completely.

You now want to stuff your pasta shells with the pumpkin filling. To do this you can either use a spoon or a piping bag. Be gentle as the shells are now quite delicate — if you lose a couple don't worry as you should have plenty of pasta.

For the pecorino sauce

80 g (2¾ oz/scant 1 cup) freshly
  grated pecorino cheese
125 g (4½ oz/½ cup) sheep's milk
  yoghurt
a dash of lemon juice
a tiny pinch of chilli flakes
salt and freshly ground black pepper
pouring (whipping) cream or milk
  (optional)

For serving

45 ml (1½ fl oz) extra virgin olive oil
a few ligurian olives
2 large very ripe ox-heart or
  beefsteak tomatoes, chopped
1 bunch of basil
a wedge of pecorino cheese

To make the pecorino sauce, put the pecorino and yoghurt in a bowl and season with the lemon, chilli, salt and pepper. Combine everything together until you have a smooth paste. You are looking for a thick sauce, so you may need to adjust the consistency with a little cream or milk.

To serve, put the oil in a large frying pan, add the olives and place over a high heat; as the pan heats up the olives will begin to fry and their juices will start to come out — when this happens add the chopped tomatoes and allow them to heat through.

Add your filled pasta shells to the pan and turn down to a gentle heat. Use your eye to tell you how much moisture is required in the pan, this will depend largely on the tomatoes: you may need to add a little water to keep the pan moist, but not too much so the sauce is thin and watery. Put on the lid, then cook the pasta for 8–10 minutes, just long enough for the flavours to infuse and the pasta to heat up — you will need to gently stir from time to time to ensure everything heats evenly and make sure they don't stick.

Just before serving tear up the basil and toss it through the pasta. Transfer the pasta to your plates and finish with a dollop of the pecorino sauce. Use a vegetable peeler to shave shards of pecorino cheese over the top.

Orechiette with broccoli, bitter greens and pecorino cheese

Serves 6

I love it when you discover a recipe that takes an everyday ingredient such as broccoli and turns it into a flavour that leaves you making appreciative noises after each mouthful. Pay close attention to the browning of the garlic in this recipe — when you get it 'just so' you will create an amazing nutty flavour that carries along wonderfully with the broccoli.

1 bunch of cavolo nero or other bitter green leaf

1 bunch of rocket (arugula)

2 heads of broccoli

1 bunch of broccoli sprouts or broccolini

100 ml (3½ fl oz) extra virgin olive oil

4 cloves of garlic, crushed and 2 cloves of garlic, thinly sliced

a good pinch of chilli flakes

2 anchovy fillets

500 ml (17 fl oz/2 cups) dry white wine

500 g (1 lb 2 oz) good-quality orechiette or casarecci pasta

300 g (10½ oz/3⅓ cups) freshly grated pecorino cheese

Chop the cavolo nero and rocket together. Slice off the broccoli florets as close to the flower as possible and cut the florets to the same size as the pasta. Then peel and slice the stem into 1 cm (½ inch) pieces. Cut the broccoli sprouts to the same size as the pasta.

Heat half of the oil in a saucepan and gently fry the crushed garlic and half of the chilli flakes until golden and tender. Add the anchovy fillets and the raw sliced broccoli stems and cook for 2–3 minutes. Pour in the white wine and cook until the broccoli is tender and the wine has all but cooked away, about 10–12 minutes. Scoop the mixture into a blender and blend until smooth, then set aside.

Bring a large pot of salted water to boil. Have a large frying pan next to it because once you begin cooking you want to have everything you need in place. When the water has started to boil, blanch the broccoli florets and broccolini. After 2 minutes lift the vegetables out of the water with a slotted spoon and let sit on a plate until you have everything else ready.

Now drop the orecchiette into the same water as the vegetables. While the pasta is cooking (about 10–12 minutes) you want to finish your sauce. In your frying pan cook the sliced garlic and remaining chilli flakes in the rest of the olive oil until toasted and a 'nutty' aroma is released. Add your chopped cavolo nero and rocket and allow to wilt slightly. Add your broccoli sauce, blanched broccolini and broccoli. You may want to splash in some water to help combine things nicely but don't add too much as you want this to be a fairly dry sauce.

By now your pasta should be cooked and you simply lift your pasta out of the water using a slotted spoon or sieve, drop it into your pan of sauce and toss about. Add most of the pecorino, reserving some to sprinkle over the top of the finished dish.

Ketchup

Makes 800 ml (28 fl oz)

6 green apples, peeled, cored and
  roughly chopped
3 red capsicums (peppers), halved,
  seeded and roughly chopped
3 brown onions, finely sliced
10 roma (plum) tomatoes, blanched
  and peeled, roughly chopped
115 ml (3¾ fl oz) cider vinegar
12 garlic cloves
1 teaspoon black peppercorns
1 teaspoon allspice
1 teaspoon ground cloves
1 teaspoon fennel seeds
½ teaspoon cayenne pepper
200 g (7 oz) soft brown sugar
150 g (5½ oz) caster (superfine)
  sugar
salt

Put the apple, capsicum, onion and tomato in a food processor and process to make a smooth purée. Transfer to a saucepan and cook over low heat for about 20 minutes, or until reduced to a sauce consistency.

Meanwhile, put the vinegar, garlic and spices in a small saucepan over high heat and cook until reduce by two-thirds, or until the aromas have infused the vinegar. Add the vinegar to the tomato sauce and cook for about 20–30 minutes, or until reduced again.

Once the sauce has thickened slightly, add the brown and caster sugars, season with salt and stir until the sugar has dissolved and the mixture is smooth Taste and adjust the seasoning if necessary. Pour into sterilised airtight jars and seal when cool. Ketchup can be stored in the refrigerator for up to 1 month.

Tomato base

Makes about 400 g (14 oz)

2 kg (4 lb 8 oz) of the very ripest
tomatoes you can get
1 bulb of garlic, cut in half (you
don't need to peel the cloves)
300 ml (10½ fl oz) extra virgin olive
oil
1 bunch of thyme
a few sprigs of basil
a little sugar (you can taste and
adjust later on)
salt and freshly ground black pepper
a splash of balsamic vinegar

Preheat your oven to 170°C (325°F/Gas 3). Chop the tomatoes and put in a roasting tin with all the other ingredients, then place in the oven. During the cooking process stir and mash the tomatoes often, being sure to stir any dark pieces through the sauce — you want the tomatoes to colour, but be careful not to let them burn or there will be a nasty bitter flavour. The length of cooking time will vary on a how 'wet' your tomatoes are but will probably take 2–2½ hours. You are looking for a thick, oily sauce.

When you are happy with your sauce remove from the oven and allow it to cool slightly, then push through a mouli — do not blend. I know it is easier to use a blender but the result is inferior. If you don't have a mouli you can push the sauce through a very fine strainer or a coarse strainer lined with muslin (cheesecloth). Taste for seasoning and once completely cool, store in a jar in the fridge. This will keep for at least a month.

Tomato dressing

Makes 350 ml (12 fl oz)

3 large, perfectly ripe ox-heart
tomatoes, coarsely chopped
2 anchovy fillets
45 ml (1½ fl oz) red wine vinegar
(an aged vinegar is preferable)
salt and freshly ground black pepper
185 ml (6 fl oz / ¾ cup) extra virgin
olive oil (the best you've got in the
cupboard)

Put the tomatoes, anchovies, vinegar and salt and pepper into a blender and purée — ox-heart tomatoes will purée to juice really easily. When the tomatoes have blended to a juice, strain off all of the solids, then whisk in the oil. Your dressing should be quite thin and not too oily. Taste the dressing and adjust the seasoning and vinegar as required. You'll be using a lot of dressing for each serve so you want the flavour to be generous but not too overpowering — think along the lines of a well-flavoured tomato juice.

Confit tomato

1 litre (35 fl oz/4 cups) extra virgin
  olive oil
12 roma (plum) tomatoes
herb stalks, the more the merrier

Preheat your oven to 120°C (235°F/Gas ½). Pour the oil into a roasting tin and put in the oven for 10 minutes to warm. Add the tomatoes to the hot oil and return to the oven. Cook for about 12 minutes or until just starting to soften. You want the tomato to just start to cook down, but to be kept together in the skin — don't panic if the skin does split, it just means that you need to be extra gentle. Remove from the heat and allow to cool in the oil. Put the tomatoes and oil in a sterilised airtight jar; they will keep in the fridge for a couple of weeks.

Serve with bacon hash (see page 106) or the lamb shoulder and cardamom curry (see page 122). You can also just simply serve the confit broken onto a slice of toasted sourdough bread.

Potatoes fried in red wine and coriander seeds

Serves 6–8

This is a wonderful potato dish that is full of flavour. I find that if I am serving it as a side it works best with goat or lamb, as the wine and spices give the potatoes a good, strong flavour that is hard to match.

500 g (1 lb 2 oz) whole, pre-boiled chat or nicola potatoes
400 ml (14 fl oz) olive oil
25 g (1 oz/⅓ cup) coriander seeds, toasted and ground
2 tablespoons black peppercorns, toasted and ground
250 ml (9 fl oz/1 cup) red wine
salt

You will get the best results if you have a saucepan large enough to fit all of the potatoes in a single layer, but it won't matter too much if your pan isn't large enough to accommodate all the potatoes. Take your boiled potatoes and gently press until the skin splits.

Start by heating the oil until nice and hot but not smoking — the best way to test the oil is to place the handle of a wooden spoon into your oil and see if there are any bubbles rising. When the oil is ready, add your potatoes and fry until a golden colour is reached, then carefully turn the potatoes over and fry the other side. Very carefully add your spices and red wine, adding the wine in splashes to start with to avoid the oil boiling over the side of your pan. Keep cooking the potatoes on a high heat until all of the wine has evaporated and the potatoes start to fry once more. The wine will make the potatoes look quite dark but don't panic. When they are ready, gently lift them out of the oil and let them drain on paper towel. Season with salt.

Salsa verde

Makes 500 ml (17 fl oz/2 cups)

1 bunch of flat-leaf (Italian) parsley, leaves picked
1 bunch of basil, leaves picked
1 bunch of chervil, leaves picked
1 bunch of chives
120 g (4¼ oz/1 cup) chopped pickled vegetables (either bought cornichons or home-made pickled cauliflower from page 234)
about 325 ml (11 fl oz) extra virgin olive oil
salt and freshly ground black pepper

Use a very sharp knife to chop your herbs; resist the temptation to use a blender as it will bruise the herbs rather than chop them. I prefer mine to be coarsely chopped as you can then pick up the individual flavours of the herbs.

Put all the herbs and the pickled vegetables in a bowl and then stir in your olive oil until the salsa verde is just wet enough to slide off your spoon; finish by tasting and adding salt and pepper as required. The sala verde is best served as soon as it is made, but it will easily keep for a few days in the fridge. Serve with the whole poached salmon (see page 169).

Pesto

Makes 350 g (12 oz/1⅓ cups)

1 bunch basil, leaves picked
2 tablespoons toasted pine nuts
60 g (2¼ oz) parmesan cheese, grated
80 ml (2½ fl oz/⅓ cup) extra virgin olive oil
salt and freshly ground black pepper

Put the basil leaves, pine nuts, parmesan and oil in a food processor and process to make a paste. Season well with salt and pepper. Alternatively you can use a mortar and pestle to grind the ingredients together. Store the pesto in an airtight container in the refrigerator for up to 2 weeks.

Parsley sauce

Makes 500 ml (17 fl oz/2 cups)

500 ml (17 fl oz/2 cups) milk
½ an onion, peeled
a couple of black peppercorns
1 bay leaf
60 g (2¼ oz) butter
2 tablespoons plain (all-purpose)
   flour
a small knob of butter, extra
½ bunch of curly parsley, chopped
salt and freshly ground black pepper

You need to make a béchamel sauce — to do this start by warming the milk, onion, peppercorns and bay leaf together in a saucepan as this will allow the flavours to infuse. Strain the milk.

While this is happening melt the butter in a second saucepan, then add the flour and combine using a wooden spoon. Cook this mixture, called a roux, over a gentle heat for about 5 minutes, then start adding the warm, infused milk a little at a time. Each time you add some milk stir until completely incorporated before adding more. To start with the mixture will look a little like a blob of paste, but it will thin with each addition of milk—keep going until all of the milk is added. Let this cook over a gentle heat for about 5 minutes.

Give the first saucepan a quick rinse, then add a knob of butter and place on a low heat. When the butter is melted add the parsley and cook while stirring for about 2–3 minutes. When the parsley has started to soften, strain your béchamel sauce onto the parsley, taste for seasoning and cook for about 1 minute further.

Serve immediately with the corned beef and buttered vegetables (see page 116).

Pickled cauliflower, carrots or whatever

Makes 2 litres (70 fl oz/8-cups)

If you are going to pickle anything always do more than you need. That way you have plenty of leftovers. Once you feel confident with the basics of pickling, it is time to experiment with some other vegetables. There are a few basic guidelines for success. Hard root vegetables such as carrots, kohlrabi and swede (rutabaga) should be partially cooked before adding to a cool brine. Beetroots (beets) should be cooked whole in the brine (use the quantities below but add an extra 200 ml/7 fl oz of water), then peeled afterwards. Cucumbers and zucchini (courgettes) need only be immersed in the cool brine, then left for at least 48 hours. Slicing, peeling and seeding is a matter of personal preference. Pickled vegetables will keep in the fridge for at least 1 month.

For the pickling brine
330 ml (11¼ fl oz /1⅓ cups) white wine vinegar
400 ml (14 fl oz) dry white wine
500 ml (17 fl oz /2 cups) water
325 ml (11 fl oz) extra virgin olive oil
80 ml (2½ fl oz /⅓ cup) mustard seed oil, optional
4 large red chillies, split but left whole
16 black peppercorns
8 cloves
8 allspice berries
a touch of freshly grated nutmeg
1 bunch of thyme
12 bay leaves
4 stalks of rosemary
a good pinch of salt and double that of sugar

For the pickles
1 cauliflower (about 1 kg /2 lb 4 oz), cut into florets, or
3 bunches of baby carrots, peeled (I like to leave about 1 cm (½ in) of stalk on, purely for the look— if some of the stalks fall off it doesn't really matter)

To make the pickling brine, put all the ingredients together in a small saucepan and bring to the boil over a high heat. Continue to boil for 10 minutes — you should end up with about 1.25 litres (44 fl oz/5 cups) of brine. Remove the pan from the heat.

To pickle the vegetables, put the cauliflower florets in a large bowl (at least 2 litres/70 fl oz/8-cup capacity) that is large enough to take the vegetables and all of the brine. Pour the hot brine over the florets. Take a piece of plastic wrap or baking paper and place it on top of the cauliflower to ensure that everything remains submerged. Allow to cool completely, then transfer to a sterilised 2 litre (70 fl oz/ 8 cup) jar or airtight container and store in the fridge. For best results allow the cauliflower to sit for at least 24 hours before eating.

To pickle the carrots, bring a large saucepan of salted water to the boil and cook the carrots for about 2–3 minutes. When you test a carrot, it should be very crunchy and only half cooked. Strain and run under cold water until completely cool. Allow the brine to cool completely, then pour it over the cooked carrots. They are now ready to store either in a sterilised 2 litre (70 fl oz /8-cup) jar or an airtight container. They are best stored for at least 48 hours before eating.

Zucchini fritters

4 large zucchini (courgettes)
salt
2 eggs, beaten
140 g (5 oz/heaped 1 cup) plain
   (all-purpose) flour
a pinch of salt
a tiny pinch of chilli flakes
vegetable oil, for frying

Grate the zucchini, then season with a little salt and allow to drain for about 30 minutes. Squeeze out as much of the liquid as you can from the zucchini, then place into a bowl with the egg, flour, salt and chilli. Mix together into a batter.

Heat a large frying pan with about 2 cm (¾ inch) of vegetable oil over medium–high heat and add dollops of the zucchini mixture, a tablespoon at a time. When golden on one side, flip them over and cook the other side. When they are ready, lift out of the pan and place onto paper towel to drain. Repeat with the rest of the zucchini batter until all cooked. These fritters go well served on the side of soups instead of bread.

Tempuring

Makes ½ cup

300 ml (10½ fl oz) vegetable oil
5 large red chillies, thinly sliced
1 bunch of curry leaves
10 cloves of garlic, thinly sliced
5 French shallots, thinly sliced
60 g (2¼ oz) salt

Heat the oil in a deep saucepan. Check the temperature of the oil before you start cooking — to do this you dip a wooden spoon into the oil and when you see that little bubbles are forming around the spoon your oil is hot enough and you can start cooking. You need to cook everything separately and when they just start to become crisp use a slotted spoon to remove onto crumpled paper towels to drain. Be careful when deep-frying the curry leaves, as they will spit fiercely for the first second of cooking. Start with the chilli, then the curry leaves, garlic, and finally, the shallots.

Gently toss everything together and season with salt. Store in an airtight container for up to 1 month. Tempuring can be used to liven up a piece of steamed fish, garnish a salad or sprinkle over the top of the lamb shoulder and cardamom curry on pages 122–123.

Pumpkin pie

Serves 8–10

This is a classic recipe. For those of you who think that pumpkin should only be eaten as a savoury food, you have obviously never been enchanted by a well-spiced pumpkin pie! To personalise this recipe you can grate a small piece of ginger into your pie filling just before baking or use some maple syrup to replace some of the sugar.

For the pastry

185 g (6½ oz/1½ cups) plain (all-purpose) flour

1 teaspoon salt

120 g (4¼ oz) cold unsalted butter, diced small

4–6 tablespoons ice cold water

For the filling

3 eggs

185 g (6½ oz/1 cup) soft brown sugar

1 teaspoon ground cinnamon

½ teaspoon ground ginger

¼ teaspoon freshly ground cloves

½ teaspoon salt

500 g (1 lb 2 oz/2 cups) cooked, mashed pumpkin (winter squash) (you'll need to cook about 1.4 kg/ 3 lb 2 oz pumpkin)

230 ml (7¾ fl oz) pouring (whipping) cream

Sift the flour and the salt in a bowl, then add the butter and, using a pastry cutter or a fork, cut the butter into the flour until the butter is about half the size of a pea. Start to add a little of the water and use a fork to mix it in, then use your hands and work until you have a firm, but not hard, dough. Don't add too much water or your dough will be sticky and hard to use, and also the finished pastry will be too tough. Form your dough into a ball, cover in plastic wrap and allow to rest for about 2 hours.

Grease a 28 cm (11¼ inch) pie tin. Turn your pastry out onto a floured board and, using a rolling pin, roll the pastry until it is about 3 mm (⅛ inches) thick. Carefully roll your pastry around your rolling pin to gently lift it into your pie tin. Gently press the pastry into place with your fingers. Allow this to rest for about 30 minutes in the fridge. Preheat your oven to 180°C (350°F/Gas 4). Cover the pastry with baking paper, fill with baking beads and blind bake for 15 minutes.

Increase the oven temperature to 210°C (415°F/Gas 6–7). To make the filling, lightly beat the eggs in a large bowl, then add your sugar, spices, salt and mashed pumpkin and mix well. Lastly, add the cream and mix well. Taste your mixture for seasoning and then simply pour into your prepared pie shell and bake in the oven for 40–45 minutes, or until the tip of a knife inserted into the filling comes out clean. Remove from the oven and allow to cool before removing from the pie tin and slicing into pieces. I rarely serve this with anything other than whipped cream.

Fruit Basket

Basket

Sour cherry and apple parfait

Serves 8

This is a great, easy recipe with no churning required. It also demonstartes the very simple technique of making a frozen parfait.

150 ml (5 fl oz) dry white wine

160 g (5¾ oz/⅔ cup) caster (superfine) sugar

4 golden delicious apples, peeled, cored and quartered

1 cinnamon stick

1 tablespoon Calvados

50 g (1¾ oz) dried sour cherries or dried cranberries

3 egg yolks

150 ml (5 fl oz) pouring (whipping) cream

a few amaretti biscuits (cookies), to serve (optional)

Place the wine and 80 g (2¾ oz/⅓ cup) of the sugar in a saucepan over medium–low heat and warm to dissolve the sugar, then add your apple and cinnamon, cover with a lid and cook gently until the apple is soft. Remove the cinnamon, transfer to a food processor and blend until completely smooth. While you are blending, add the Calvados. Place the apple purée into a bowl, then add the sour cherries.

Place the egg yolks and remaining sugar into a separate bowl and whisk until thick, pale and creamy. Place your cream into a third large bowl and whisk until you have soft peaks. Fold the egg yolks, then the apple into the cream.

Pour this mixture into one large container to freeze for at least 6 hours or overnight. Remember to pull it out of the freezer about 20 minutes before you want to serve to allow it to soften a little.

Scoop your parfait into individual bowls or glasses, then crumble over the amaretti biscuit if desired.

Banana jam

Makes about 500 g (1 lb 2 oz)

When you make this recipe a couple of times you will notice that the colour will vary quite a bit from red-brown to pale yellow. This seems to have soemthing to do with the ripeness of the fruit and how long the bananas have been stored for. Pay attention to your tastebuds when making this jam and be prepared for a surprise with the colour.

600 ml (21 fl oz) orange juice
a squeeze of lemon juice
340 g (11¾ oz/1½ cups) caster
  (superfine) sugar
2 kg (4 lb 8 oz) slightly over-ripe
  bananas

Put the orange juice, lemon juice and sugar in a large saucepan and bring to the boil. While the juice is boiling, break pieces of banana into the pan and stir continuously. Continue to boil for no longer than 15 minutes, at which stage the mixture should be pulpy and jammy.

Place the jam into sterilised airtight jars and seal when cool. The banana jam can then be stored in the refrigerator for about 2 weeks.

Fresh berries with crème de framboise and clotted cream

Serves 4–6

I think that we are all familiar with fresh berries, aren't we? Well then, what about clotted cream? I know the name doesn't exactly sound appealing but, trust me, it is fantastic. It has the texture of soft butter and a wonderful slightly waxy and buttery flavour. The best thing is that the less you do to it the better — in fact, if you try to mix the cream too much it will lose its natural thick but light consistency. There is no trick or mystery to this dish — you should only buy berries that you have had an opportunity to sample first to ensure that their flavour is worthy enough, but the type of berries you select is completely up to you. If all you can get is strawberries then so be it; if you can get hold of a wide selection of beautiful berries then all the better. I like to use crème de framboise to marinate the berries but you can substitute this for any berry-flavoured liquor.

550 g (1 lb 4 oz) fresh berries
150 ml (5 fl oz) crème de framboise
a touch of sugar
a few leaves of mint
150 g (5½ oz) clotted cream

Do as little as possible to the berries (such as removing the green tops from the strawberries) and only cut them if it is absolutely necessary. All you need to do is place your berries into a large bowl, then pour in the crème de framboise, add a little sugar and then sprinkle in a few mint leaves. Gently toss to ensure that the berries are well coated and leave this in the fridge for an hour or two. When you are ready to serve, either spoon the berries into individual dishes or pour into a large serving bowl, making sure to drizzle in all of the liquor, then top with dollops of the clotted cream.

Baked rhubarb

Serves 4

350 g (12 oz) rhubarb, leaves removed, stems washed and cut into 4 cm (1½ inch) pieces
230 g (8 oz/1 cup) caster (superfine) sugar
juice of 1 orange

Put the rhubarb on a tray and sprinkle with half of the sugar. Gently toss about to make sure that the rhubarb is well covered in the sugar, then set aside for at least 4 hours, but preferably overnight.

Preheat your oven to 150°C (300°F/Gas 2). Place the rhubarb in a roasting tin — don't stack it on top of each other but allow a little space between. Sprinkle with the remaining sugar and drizzle with the orange juice. Bake for 35 minutes, or until the rhubarb has shrivelled a little but is not overcooked.

Serve straight away with the panna cotta on page 60, or it's also great on cereal. For something a bit different, make soft polenta on milk, sweeten it slightly and serve with the baked rhubarb for breakfast.

How to cook quinces

Quince are a wonderful fruit in season and once prepared and cooked they will last for a few months in the fridge. These cooked quinces are used in the orange and quince cake (see page 258) but can just as easily be served in a serving bowl with a blob of clotted cream alongside, then drizzled with a little of the quince syrup before crumbling an amaretti biscuit (cookie) over the top for an easy dessert.

Quinces are very hard, which makes them difficult to cut so it is important to use a sharp knife and be very careful. Start by peeling 2 kg (4 lb 8 oz) quinces using a sharp vegetable peeler, then carefully cut the quinces into quarters and remove the cores. Reserve all of the peeling and cores and place them onto a large piece of muslin (cheesecloth) or a clean tea towel (dish towel), then roll up into a parcel and tie up securely with twine.

Preheat your oven to 180°C (350°F/Gas 4). Choose a large saucepan that will be able to go into a hot oven. Prepare your cooking liquid by combining 1 kg (2 lb 4 oz/ 4½ cups) sugar, 2 litres (70 fl oz/8 cups) water, 2 cinnamon sticks, the zest and juice of 1 lemon and 1 orange, 4 cloves, 2 bay leaves, 10 peppercorns and 500 ml (17 fl oz/ 2 cups) red wine in a saucepan. Bring it up to the boil, then carefully add the prepared quinces, then add the parcel of cores and seeds to help keep your quinces under the liquid. Bring this up to a simmer and then place into the oven for anywhere from 3–5 hours. What you will notice is that as they are cooking, the quince will start off pale and hard, then it will turn pale and very soft — during this stage do not stir the fruit or it will break up.

About halfway through cooking it will start to become pink, then, as it cooks further it will start to deepen in colour to burgundy red and the flesh will start to firm up slightly. When you are at this stage, remove the quinces from the oven and allow to cool completely in the liquid.

Remove the fruit and place into a large jar or container. Place the liquid back on the heat and bring to the boil, reduce the liquid by a third, then remove from the heat and allow to cool. When the syrup is completely cold, strain it back over the fruit. The fruit should be completely covered by the liquid, and this will preserve the fruit for a few months in the fridge.

Pickled and spiced cherries

Makes 2.5 litres (87 fl oz/10 cups)

For the best results here you need to have patience, which I find to be the most difficult thing. I get really excited when the cherry season starts and my produce supplier gets a little frustrated about my need for a constant cherry update. Are they any good? What size are they? How much are they per box? When I feel they are perfect, usually about 5 to 7 weeks after the first box goes on sale, I start to pickle as many as I can. There is a nice annual tradition at my local vegetable markets to auction off the first box of cherries of the season and donate the proceeds to charity.

1 kg (2 lb 4 oz) cherries, left intact, with the stems on
750 ml (26 fl oz /3 cups) red wine vinegar
500 g (1 lb 2 oz /2¾ cups) soft brown sugar
6 cloves
6 juniper berries
4 allspice berries
1 star anise
the peel and juice of 1 lemon, peel cut into strips
1 stick of cinnamon
2 green cardamom pods

Pick through the cherries for any less than perfect ones, then give them a rinse. Put all the other ingredients in a large saucepan and bring to the boil. Boil for about 5 minutes, then add your cherries and cook for a further 5 minutes before removing the pan from the heat. Allow to sit overnight before transferring everything into sterilised jars. These will keep for months.

Pomegranate salad

Serves 4–6

80 g (2¾ oz) French shallots, finely chopped
a pinch of salt
a pinch of sugar
freshly ground black pepper
80 ml (2½ fl oz/⅓ cup) white vinegar
150 ml (5 fl oz) extra virgin olive oil
3 large pomegranates
150 ml (5 fl oz) pomegranate molasses
1 small handful of mixed chopped mint and chopped flat-leaf (Italian) parsley

Place the finely chopped shallots into a small bowl and season with the salt, sugar, pepper and vinegar. Leave this to sit for about 20 minutes to allow the shallot to pickle slightly. Whisk in the oil, then check that you are happy with the seasoning and adjust as needed.

To prepare the pomegranates, cut the fruit in half and place the cut side of the pomegranate down onto the palm of your hand. Working over a bowl to catch the seeds, whack the tough skin of the pomegranate to shake out all of the seeds. Add the rest of the ingredients to the seeds, stir well and season to taste.

This is good served with the roast lamb leg with avocado and pitta bread (see page 137).

Lemon and mint granita

Serves 8

This is an extremely simple frozen dessert and one that is delicious and refreshing. The other great thing is that it takes very little effort to experiment with other flavours. How about adding a little gin? Perhaps some lemoncello? Or what about infusing the water with something other than mint?

1 litre (35 fl oz/4 cups) water
320 g (11¼ oz/1½ cups) sugar
1 bunch of mint
200 ml (7 fl oz) lemon juice
shredded mint, extra

Put the water and sugar together in a saucepan and bring to a boil. Once it has boiled, add the bunch of mint and lemon juice and allow to cool completely. Strain the liquid through a fine sieve to remove all of the solids, then taste the syrup. When food is frozen it is slightly harder for your taste buds to pick up on some of the flavours, which means that when you taste the liquid at this stage you want it to be slightly too sweet and too lemony.

When you are happy with the flavour of the syrup, pour into a container and place in the freezer for at least 24 hours. When you remove the granita from the freezer it will be a solid block of ice, so what you want to do now is use a fork to start to scrape and 'fluff up' the surface of the granita. Serve in chilled glasses, garnished with a little extra mint.

Pineapple with cream and ginger nut biscuits

Serves 4

A very simple recipe that is best when pineapples are at their peak. You've got my mum to thank for this recipe, which is based on one of my favourite childhood desserts. The simple version is a ginger nut biscuit warmed in a muffin tin in the oven; when the biscuit becomes soft you use the back of a spoon to push down on the biscuit to make little ginger nut bowls. Then top with whipped cream and some chopped pineapple. The recipe below is nothing more than a fancy version of mum's dessert.

1 pineapple
2 tablespoons caster (superfine)
  sugar, plus 1 tablespoon extra
100 ml (3½ fl oz) thick (double/
  heavy) cream or goat's curd
3 ginger nut biscuits (ginger snaps)

Preheat your oven to 170°C (325°F/Gas 3). Take your pineapple and do nothing to it; if you feel you must you can cut off the leaves but do not cut into the fruit itself. Place the pineapple in the oven for 2 hours or so until it feels soft and gives a little — be sure to turn it from time to time to ensure even cooking. Add 2 tablespoons of the sugar to the cream or goat's curd.

Allow the pineapple to cool slightly, then use a sharp serrated knife to cut off the top and the bottom, then carefully cut away the skin. Cut the flesh into quarters and remove the core. Place, core side down, on a tray, sprinkle with the remaining tablespoon of sugar and, using a blowtorch (preferable) or a really hot grill (broiler), caramelize the sugar on top of the pineapple.

Transfer the pineapple to your plates, place a quenelle of sweetened cream or goat's curd next to it and, using the coarsest side of your grater, grate the biscuits over the top. If you find it easier, you could use a small food processor to chop up the ginger nut biscuits instead of using the grater.

Strawberry breast

Serves 4

This Italian dessert, also known as 'Fragomammella' has a long and interesting history and makes an impressive end to a meal. I have altered it slightly from the original by adding just a little goat's cheese to the cream — traditionally, ricotta is used.

For the strawberries

500 g (1 lb 2 oz) strawberries, stems trimmed and large ones cut in half

2 tablespoons water

1 lemon, peeled then juiced, peel reserved

250 g (9 oz/heaped 1 cup) caster (superfine) sugar

2–3 mint leaves, torn, to serve

For the cream

200 ml (7 fl oz) thick (double/heavy) cream

80 g (2¾ oz) soft goat's cheese

80 ml (2½ fl oz/⅓ cup) of the chilled strawberry syrup

You want to cook the strawberries a couple of hours in advance or even the day before. Pour the water and juice from the lemon into a large flat frying pan, then add the sugar and place over medium heat and cook until the sugar has melted and dissolved. During this process try not to stir the sugar too much, instead swirl the pan around to move the sugar about. When the sugar has started to cook, turn your heat up high and cook just until you start to get a little colour, then add the strawberries and lemon peel. The sugar will set and clump on the strawberries which is fine — try to coat the strawberries as well as you can, then remove the pan from the heat and scrape everything into a bowl.

As the strawberries cool after a couple of hours, strain off the juice and discard the lemon peel. Place the strawberries in the fridge and pour the remaining juice into a small saucepan and boil until it has reduced by half, then remove from the heat and allow to cool completely in the fridge.

Make the cream about an hour before you wish to serve the dish. Place the cream in a large bowl, then crumble your goat's cheese into small pieces and add to the bowl. Use a large whisk to fold the cheese through the cream until you just start to see ribbons. Drizzle in the cold strawberry syrup to give a soft pink hue. Use a whisk to whip until you have soft peaks but don't worry if the cheese is not completely incorporated, as you don't want to overwork the cream.

To serve, make a mound of strawberries on a platter while reserving one strawberry that looks best. Scatter over the mint. Now take your cream and using the biggest serving spoon you have, dip it in hot water and then try to get one large scoop of cream to cover the strawberries. You should have a little of the strawberry syrup left, so pour a little around the 'breast'. To finish, place on the last remaining strawberry ... you guessed it, the nipple!

Hot angelina plum tart

Serves 6

This tart is a nice, easy recipe that takes advantage of the cute shape and size of the plums and the robust flavour of their flesh, which holds up against the flavours of the butter, sugar and lemon. The tart is cooked in a similar manner to a tarte tatin.

a knob of unsalted butter
1 kg (2 lb 4 oz) ripe angelina plums
165 g (5¾ oz/⅔ cup) sugar
the finely grated zest of 1 lemon
the juice of 1 lemon
1–2 sheets of bought puff pastry

Preheat your oven to 180°C (350°F/Gas 4). Choose a flameproof pan that will fit the plums comfortably in one layer and can also go into a hot oven. In that pan melt your butter over a medium heat; when the butter starts to foam, add the plums, sugar, lemon zest and juice. Increase the heat so the pan is over a high heat and sauté the plums until the skin just starts to blister, about 2 minutes. Tip out the plums and allow to cool enough to be handled. Don't wash your pan, you will be using this again shortly.

Squeeze out the stones from the plums, trying to keep the plums as intact as possible, then arrange them back into your pan with the prettiest side on the base of the pan. Add any juice that may have come out during the stoning process.

Cut the puff pastry so it is just a little wider than your pan and place on top of your plums — you'll probably need to have two sheets overlapping to cover the whole pan. Tuck the edges of the pastry into the pan. Return the pan to the heat until the plums start to fry, then place the pan into the oven. Cook for about 50 minutes. I was once told that when you cook puff pastry you should cook it until it looks cooked, then give it another 5 minutes because there is nothing worse than half-cooked dough. Undercooked dough is usually caused by people who are nervous about colouring their pastry too much. You don't want it burnt but it does need to be well cooked in order to taste good.

Invert the tart onto a serving plate — the easiest way to do this is to hold your plate over the pan, then quickly flip the pan over. Serve with your choice of custard, cream or ice cream. The way I normally serve it is with a quenelle of thick (double/heavy) cream on top.

Cape gooseberry clafoutis with gooseberry mascarpone

Serves 8

A clafoutis is a simple batter cake that benefits from its batter being prepared the day before, as the almonds give off a better flavour if they have been allowed to infuse into the batter. But if you really have a craving and need to make the clafoutis and eat it straight away, then you will still get good results.

For the batter
100 g (3½ oz/⅔ cup) almonds, lightly toasted
25 g (1 oz/¼ cup) plain (all-purpose) flour
a pinch of salt
200 g (7 oz/scant 1 cup) caster (superfine) sugar
4 eggs and 6 yolks, lightly beaten together
250 ml (9 fl oz/1 cup) pouring (whipping) cream

For the gooseberry mascarpone
100 g (3½ oz) cape gooseberries (physalis), removed from their husks
55 g (2 oz/¼ cup) sugar
a splash of lemon juice
200 g (7 oz/scant 1 cup) mascarpone
45–80 ml (1½–2½ fl oz) pouring (whipping) cream

To cook the clafoutis
some butter, at room temperature
some caster (superfine) sugar
400 g (14 oz) cape gooseberries (physalis)

To make the batter, grind the almonds in a food processor until ground but with a few large bits remaining. Tip into a bowl. Place the flour and salt into the food processor and pulse a few times, then add the sugar and blend for a brief moment, then add the almonds and return to the processor and give another brief blend. While the blender is running, add the eggs and cream. Only blend for as long as it takes for everything to combine. Pour into a container and cover with plastic wrap, then place this in your fridge overnight.

To make the gooseberry mascarpone, put your gooseberries, sugar and lemon juice in a bowl and, using the back of a wooden spoon, crush the gooseberries into a really chunky pulp. Let this sit at room temperature for about 1 hour, then add the mascarpone and a splash of the cream and stir to combine, only adding as much as you need to combine everything into a soft cream that just holds its shape.

You can make individual clafoutis using eight ovenproof dishes about 14 cm (5½ inches) across and 1.5 cm (⅝ inches) deep. Alternatively, make one large clafoutis in a 25 cm (10 inches) ovenproof dish, about 2 cm (¾ inches) deep. Smear some of the butter over the surface of the dish(es), then spoon in the sugar and shake the dish(es) to coat the butter with sugar, then shake out any excess. Scatter in the gooseberries, then stir your batter well before pouring it in.

Clafoutis is best cooked in a fan-forced oven. If your oven is not fan-forced, increase the temperature by 10°C (20°F). Cook individual clafoutis in a preheated 210°C (415°F/Gas 6–7) oven for about 12 minutes. For a large clafoutis, cook in a preheated 190°C (375°F/Gas 5) oven for about 25 minutes. The clafoutis is ready when it is just set in the middle and golden and brown around the edges, and it should also puff up almost like a soufflé. Serve immediately with a dollop gooseberry mascarpone.

Orange and quince cake

Serves 10

This is a moist cake that can easily last for up to 2 days. This means that when you have people over and you want to dish them up something special but easy, and you want to make sure that there are enough leftovers for a tasty morning tea for yourself the next day, this is the cake for you. If you take time to boil the oranges correctly you will get a truly fantastic result. The other main component of this recipe is the quinces — you can substitute these for almost any other fruit, or even leave the fruit out of it altogether and have a simple orange cake.

2 oranges
250 g (9 oz/heaped 1 cup) caster (superfine) sugar
6 eggs
250 g (9 oz/2½ cups) ground almonds
1½ teaspoons baking powder
unsalted butter, for greasing
plain (all-purpose) flour, for dusting
8–10 cooked quince pieces (see pages 246–247)

Preheat your oven to 150°C (300°F/Gas 2). Start by placing the whole oranges into a saucepan and cover with cold water. Place onto a high heat and bring the water to a boil. As soon as it boils, strain off the water and cover with fresh cold water and then return to the heat until it boils again. Repeat this process six times, each time exchanging the boiled water for fresh cold water. What this process achieves is to gently coax the bitter, harsh flavours out of the orange skin while cooking the oranges until they are soft enough to purée. After you have tipped off the final batch of water, allow the oranges to cool enough to handle before cutting into quarters and carefully removing any seeds. Place the oranges (peel and all) into a food processor and blend really well. While the oranges are blending, add the sugar and eggs and blend some more, then add the ground almonds and baking powder and give it one more blend.

Take a 24 cm (9½ inch) spring-form tin and rub with a little butter, then add a big pinch of flour to the tin and shake the flour around until the entire surface of the tin has been coated. Arrange pieces of quince over the bottom of the tin, then pour in the orange mixture. Bake for about 1 hour, or until a skewer inserted into the centre of the cake comes out clean.

Peach and cherry casserole

Serves 8

This recipe can be changed to suit whichever summer fruits you choose. I prefer to make these in individual dishes, but it can easily be made into one larger dish to be shared.

4 small, ripe peaches
100 ml (3½ fl oz) water
300 g (10½ oz/scant 1½ cups) caster (superfine) sugar
40 cherries
the peel and juice of 1 lemon, peel cut into strips
2 vanilla beans, split down the middle into quarters
1 stick of cinnamon, gently crushed

Preheat your oven to 180°C (350°F/Gas 4). Firstly, peel your peaches — treat them the same way you would a tomato by soaking them in boiling water for a few seconds, then lifting straight into cold water. Use the tip of a knife to gently pull away the skins. Now, cut them in half and remove the stones.

Make a light caramel by boiling the water and the sugar together in a saucepan until syrupy. While this is happening put the cherries, lemon peel and juice, vanilla beans and cinnamon in a separate bowl. When the caramel has started to become a pale straw colour add all of the ingredients that are in the bowl to the pan, then remove the pan from the heat and gently fold together. This will 'stop' the caramel.

In small heatproof dishes, place a peach half and five cherries along with a piece of vanilla and cinnamon, then pour on any remaining liquid. Cover each dish with foil and bake for 10–15 minutes. Serve with a dollop of sweetened cream or ice cream.

Drunken aunties' plum trifle

Serves 6

This is one of those desserts that I have to do at Christmas purely for sentimental reasons, but it is good whenever stone fruit is in season — try replacing the plums with peaches or nectarines. I make these trifles in individual glass bowls, but you can easily make it into one large trifle.

For the jelly (gelatine dessert)
400 g (14 oz) black muscat grapes
200 g (7 oz/scant 1 cup) caster
  (superfine) sugar
½ bunch of mint
1 piece of lemon peel
4 x 2 g leaves of sheet gelatine
  (gold strength)

For the plums
45 ml (1½ fl oz) red wine
100 ml (3½ fl oz) sweet sherry
400 ml (14 fl oz) water
100 g (3½ oz/scant ½ cup) sugar
a small piece of cinnamon
6 ripe blood plums

To make the jelly, put the grapes, sugar, mint and lemon peel in a saucepan with just enough water to cover. Boil everything together for about 15–20 minutes and use a whisk or potato masher to squash the grapes as they cook. Pour into a sieve over a bowl. Place a weight on top of the cooked grapes — you want to get out as much of the juice as possible, then allow this to strain until cool. Measure the amount of liquid you have, it should yield 500 ml (17 fl oz/2 cups), but it may vary slightly. Top up with water if necessary.

Soak the gelatine in cold water to soften. While this is happening, bring your grape syrup to the boil in a saucepan, then turn off the heat. Take your softened gelatine and squeeze out any excess liquid, then add the gelatine to the grape syrup. Stir until dissolved, then pour the mixture into a 30 x 24 cm (12 x 9½ inch) baking tray. Refrigerate and allow to set; this will take at least 2 hours.

To make the plums, put the wine, sherry, water, sugar and cinnamon in a saucepan and bring to the boil. When boiling, add the plums and cook until the skin is starting to split, then lift out the plums and continue to boil the syrup until it has reduced by half. Remove the pan from the heat and allow to cool slightly. When the plums have cooled enough to touch, peel off their skins, then take a small knife and slice in half following the stone, then gently pull away the two halves and remove the stone. Put the prepared plums in a container and pour on the syrup while it is still warm, then allow to cool completely. Keep the cinnamon in for flavour but fish it out before serving.

For the sponge cake

5 large eggs, separated

dash of natural vanilla extract

225 g (8 oz/1 heaped cup) caster
(superfine) sugar

60 g (2¼ oz/½ cup) sifted plain
(all-purpose) flour

60 g (2¼ oz/½ cup) sifted cornflour
(cornstarch)

a pinch of salt

For the custard cream

100 ml (3½ fl oz) pouring
(whipping) cream

1 vanilla bean, split down the
middle

1 piece of lemon peel

3 egg yolks

50 g (1¾ oz/scant ¼ cup) caster
(superfine) sugar

80 ml (2½ fl oz/⅓ cup) thick
(double/heavy) cream

For serving

a heavy-handed splash of sherry
(think of drunken aunties)

a few mint leaves

Preheat your oven to 180°C (350°F/Gas 4). To make the sponge cake, beat the egg yolks, vanilla and sugar with a spatula until thick and creamy. Sift the flour and cornflour together and carefully fold into the egg yolk mix. Whisk the egg whites and the salt until stiff, then fold your egg yolk mixture into this. Line and flour a shallow baking tray — the size doesn't matter too much as for this recipe you can cut the sponge cake however you like but as a guide use a tray about 38 x 30 cm (15 x 12 inch) that's around 3 cm (1¼ inches) deep. Bake for 12–14 minutes, or until a toothpick inserted into the cake comes out clean. Remove from the oven and allow to cool slightly in the tin before turning out onto a wire rack and allowing to cool completely.

To make the custard cream, gently warm the cream, vanilla and lemon in a small saucepan — don't let this boil, just let the flavours infuse the milk. In a separate bowl, whisk together the yolks and sugar until pale, then add the infused cream. Return to the pan and cook over a very low heat until the custard is thick enough to coat the back of a spoon, stirring constantly. Strain into a bowl and allow to cool, discarding the vanilla and lemon. When completely cold whisk the thick cream until stiff, then fold it through the custard.

I have old-fashioned, thick clear glass trifle bowls that I use to serve this dessert, but you can use whatever you like. Individual servings are easier to make look tidy — you'll need six bowls of about 350 ml (12 fl oz). For each trifle, cut your sponge to fit into the base and a little up the side of the bowl, then splash on some sherry. Pour in some plum syrup until the sponge is well soaked. Add two plum halves, top with a dollop of custard cream and add a couple of mint leaves. Now comes the jelly. Using your eye, cut a piece of jelly that will fit over the trifle but stay within the bowl. Run a spatula under a hot tap, then slide it under the piece of jelly and quickly lift up, then slide on to the trifle. Just before serving pour over a little more sherry.

Burnt fig and balsamic jam

Makes 600 g (1 lb 5 oz)

500 g (1 lb 2 oz) dried figs, roughly
  chopped
600 g (1 lb 5 oz/2¾ cups) caster
  (superfine) sugar
185 ml (6 fl oz/¾ cup) balsamic
  vinegar

Put the figs in a bowl and pour over just enough lukewarm water to cover. Leave to soak for 2 hours, then mush them up slightly with your hands.

Heat the sugar in a heavy-based saucepan over low heat. Allow it to form a caramel, then keep cooking until the caramel starts to get a little dark. Now you are living on the edge, as in the blink of an eye your caramel will go from very dark to horrible and black — the moment you think its about to go too far is when you remove from the heat and (very carefully) add a little of the balsamic vinegar to halt the cooking. (A little warning here, the sugar you are working with is really hot and will spit and splatter, but don't be afraid, just stand a little way back and work carefully). Add the remaining vinegar a little at a time, then add the soaked figs and return to the heat, stirring from time to time until your figs have cooked into a pulpy, jammy mass. Pour into sterilised airtight jars and seal when cool. Burnt fig and balsamic jam can be stored for up to 6 months; refrigerate after opening.

Mulled wine

Serves 6

Like many food traditions, mulled wine was developed out of necessity, which in this case was the need to re-use bad or off wine. The theory was that if you added enough honey and spice to the wine, then you could drink it. But over time, mulled wine has become steeped in tradition as a Christmas drink. In Australia, it would be a bit of a punishment to drink mulled wine in the summer heat of a southern hemisphere Christmas, so let's just call it a great winter warmer. There are thousands of variations to mulled wine but I particularly love the rich, warming flavours of the version here.

125 ml (4 fl oz/½ cup) brandy
150 g (5½ oz/⅔ cup) caster
  (superfine) sugar
100 g (3½ oz) dried sour cherries
750 ml (26 fl oz/3 cups) red wine
  (don't waste anything fancy)
2 cinnamon sticks
a pinch of grated nutmeg
3–4 cloves
2 oranges, unpeeled, sliced
1 lemon, unpeeled, sliced
125 ml (4 fl oz/½ cup) weak tea

Start by placing the brandy, sugar and sour cherries in a small saucepan, place over a very gentle heat and gradually warm while stirring to dissolve the sugar. Then add the wine, spices, orange, lemon and tea and return to a very gentle heat, stirring from time to time to allow everything to warm together. Keep it on the heat until it is just about to boil, then strain into heatproof glasses and decorate with a slice of the orange.

Rhubarb mojito

Makes 1

When I was a kid, we had this great big rhubarb plant growing outside the kitchen window. One of my favourite things to do was to chop off a stalk and sit down with a little dish of sugar, dip the rhubarb into the sugar and chomp away. This drink is a play on the traditional lime-based mojito — I like the way the extremely sour rhubarb is mixed with sugar and mint. To get the most vivid colour from your rhubarb, sugar it down the day before (there is no difference in flavour). The rum you use is up to you; my preference is for Havana añejo blanco.

2 large or 3 small stalks of rhubarb
2 tablespoons sugar
4 leaves of mint
¼ lime
ice
60 ml (2 fl oz/¼ cup) white rum,
　such as añejo blanco
splash of soda water (optional)

Thinly slice the rhubarb and sprinkle it with the sugar and let it sit overnight if you wish, or you can just go straight on to making your drink.

Put the rhubarb and mint in a cocktail shaker. Squeeze in the lime juice and add the crushed lime wedge. Fill with ice to the top. Pour in the rum and shake really, really well.

Pour into a tall glass — if you need to top it up, add a splash of soda water to the cocktail shaker and wash any remaining cocktail into the glass. Serve straight away.

Pantry

Chickpea purée

Serves 8

You can use precooked and tinned chickpeas for this recipe but the flavour will not be anywhere near as good as if you soak and cook your own chickpeas. When you buy dried chickpeas they should be pale and intact. Sort through your chickpeas and remove any discoloured chickpeas. If you want to make this dip even more special, then use a really good extra virgin olive oil—something nice and peppery.

220 g (7¾ oz/1 cup) dried
  chickpeas, soaked in cold water
  for 24 hours
2 tablespoons freshly ground cumin
150 g (5½ oz) tahini
juice of 2 lemons
salt and freshly ground black pepper
115–150 ml (3¾–5 fl oz) extra
  virgin olive oil

Put the chickpeas in a saucepan with plenty of cold water and birng to the boil. Cook for at least 2½ hours, or until the chickpeas are very tender. It is very important not to salt the water at all or the chickpeas will not become tender no matter how much you cook them.

When the chickpeas are cooked, drain them, reserving about 60 ml (2 fl oz/¼ cup) of the cooking liquid. Place the chickpeas in a blender and process with the reserved cooking liquid until smooth, then add the cumin, tahini, most of the lemon juice and some salt and pepper. While the blender is running, slowly pour in 115 ml (3¾ fl oz) of olive oil, then stop the blender and taste for seasoning and consistency. When you are tasting, keep in mind that the cumin flavour will become slightly stronger as it sits, and that the consistency should be soft. If you think it needs the remainder of the oil and lemon juice, add it now. The dip is ready to serve but if you want a much finer purée, then pass through the smallest plate on a mouli.

To serve, place a dollop of the chickpea purée on a plate, make a well in the centre and drizzle in some oil. Serve alongside flatbread or crackers with wedges of lemon.

Pantry pasta

Everything used to make this dish comes from the cupboard except for the parsley. It is a good all-rounder, especially when you are busy and don't have time to shop or are caught out with unexpected guests and need to rustle up something at the last minute.

250 g (9 oz) spaghetti

200 ml (7 fl oz) extra virgin olive oil

4 cloves of garlic, sliced

16 anchovy fillets

4 red chillies, seeded and chopped or a pinch of dried chilli flakes

60 g (2¼ oz/⅓ cup) soaked and rinsed capers

1 handful flat-leaf (Italian) parsley, chopped (optional)

juice of 2 lemons

4 handfuls toasted fresh breadcrumbs (see page 297)

200 g (7 oz/2 cups) grated parmesan cheese

Bring a large saucepan of salted water to the boil. Add the spaghetti and cook for about 8–10 minutes, or until al dente — stir the spaghetti twice during cooking to ensure the pasta doesn't stick together. Drain well.

Heat the olive oil in a large frying pan over medium heat. Add the garlic and anchovies and cook until the garlic just starts to colour. Add the chilli and the capers, stir to combine, and continue cooking until the chilli darkens. Add the cooked spaghetti to the pan, toss well to combine, then season with salt and freshly ground black pepper.

Add your parsley, if using, lemon juice, breadcrumbs and parmesan cheese and toss really well before serving.

Danks Street Depot's really good nuts

Serves 4

The name says it all really — this is a recipe that was preceded by loads of failures until I got it perfect. I hope that I have taken out a lot of the hard work for you with this selection of nuts and spices. The nuts should be spicy, but not hot; sweet and salty, but not too much so; and, most of all, they should be crispy. One of the other great pleasures of this recipe is that if you crumble the cinnamon into pieces, it will cook in with the nuts and will be sweet and crispy, which means that every now and then you get this beautiful cinnamon burst.

500 ml (17 fl oz/2 cups) water
500 g (1 lb 2 oz/2¼ cups) sugar
3 cinnamon sticks
4 star anise
1½ teaspoons chilli flakes
55 g (2 oz/¼ cup) salt
200 g (7 oz/2 cups) walnuts
100 g (3½ oz/⅔ cup) almonds
100 g (3½ oz/scant ⅔ cup)
  macadamia nuts
100 g (3½ oz/⅔ cup) cashew nuts
100 g (3½ oz/⅔ cup) hazelnuts
100 g (3½ oz/⅔ cup) pistachio nuts
100 g (3½ oz/⅔ cup) peanuts
2 litres (70 fl oz/8 cups) oil
chilli powder, for seasoning
salt, for seasoning

You need to have a large heavy-based saucepan to get the best results, but I have also had success in a non-stick electric frying pan with a high lip.

Put the water, sugar, cinnamon, star anise, chilli flakes and salt in your saucepan and bring to the boil. Add all the nuts. Bring to the boil once again, then thoroughly strain the syrup from the nuts and allow to cool for about 30 minutes. (If you have the time you can let the nuts soak in the syrup overnight before straining, which will produce a much better flavour.) The nuts must be quite dry before being fried or the oil will splatter dramatically.

Half-fill a large, clean heavy-based saucepan with the oil and heat until it reaches about 170°C (325°F), or until the handle of the wooden spoon dipped in the oil starts to bubble. Carefully lower the nuts, in batches, into the oil and deep-fry each batch for 5–10 minutes until the nuts are a deep golden brown colour, stirring continuously the whole time.

When the nuts are nice and brown, remove them from the oil and place onto a clean dry tea towel (dish towel) over a tray to drain off the excess oil. As the nuts are cooling, stir them from time to time to stop them from clumping together. Allow to cool completely, then season with chilli powder and extra salt.

Re-fried beans

Serves 6

This is probably one of the most under-appreciated dishes around; it seems that beans are constantly cooked without care and served with corn chips under some stringy cheese, often found in the company of discoloured avocados and under-ripe tomatoes — such an undignified end for something as wonderful as the pinto bean!

300 g (10½ oz) dried pinto or red
  kidney beans
2 onions, chopped
4 tomatoes, chopped
4 cloves of garlic, 2 cloves left
  whole and 2 cloves diced
100 g (3½ oz) piece of pork
  back-fat, diced
1 large dried red chilli
1 dried bird's eye chilli
salt
1 bunch coriander, leaves picked
  and chopped

Check through your beans to make sure that they are in good condition and that there are no stones, then place in a bowl, cover with plenty of cold water and leave to soak overnight.

Strain the beans and place in a large saucepan with half of the onion, the tomato and 2 whole garlic cloves. Pour in enough cold water to cover, bring to the boil, then reduce the heat to low and simmer for about 45 minutes, or until the beans are really soft. You may need to add more water to keep the beans submerged, but try to make sure that when the beans are cooked they are not swimming in liquid. You should have just enough liquid left in the pan to keep the beans moist, as you do not want to strain off any flavour.

Put the pork into a large heavy-based frying pan over medium heat and allow the fat to render out. Add the remaining onion, garlic and the dried chillies, season well with salt and cook until the onion is soft and just starting to colour. Add a couple of spoonfuls of the cooked beans to the pork in the pan and use a potato masher to coarsely mash them together. Add more beans, tomato and onion and mash some more, and continue adding the remaining bean mixture until it is all incorporated, making sure you do not mash it all smooth — the idea is that some of the beans are whole and some are mashed, resulting in a pot of well-seasoned beans with loads of texture. Just before serving, taste again for seasoning and stir through the coriander.

Toasted couscous and almond salad

120 g (4¼ oz/¾ cup) blanched almonds
100 ml (3½ fl oz) olive oil
1 tablespoon cumin seeds
250 g (9 oz/1⅓ cups) couscous
350 ml (12 fl oz) chicken stock or water, boiling
salt and ground black pepper
¼ bunch of flat-leaf (Italian) parsley, chopped
1 preserved lemon, flesh and pith discarded, skin diced as finely as possible
2 tomatoes, finely diced

For this recipe you will need a saucepan with a tight-fitting lid. Place your almonds onto your chopping board and, using the flat of your knife, break into irregular pieces, but try not to crush them into a powder.

Put the oil, cumin and almonds in the saucepan over high heat and toast until you have a very light brown colour. Add the couscous and continue to toast everything until the couscous has started to turn light brown. Pour in your boiling stock or water in one go, stir a couple of times and cover with a lid as quickly as you can. Turn off the heat and allow your couscous to sit undisturbed for 10–12 minutes, then remove the lid and, using a fork, fluff up the couscous to remove any lumps; keep working until it is all nice and loose, taste and season accordingly. If you leave the lid on, the couscous will stay warm for about 20 minutes, or you can reheat it in the microwave or serve at room temperature.

When you are just about to serve, add the parsley, preserved lemon and tomato and fluff up once more.

How to make your house dressing

It's seriously easy to make your own salad dressing. In fact, I thought it was too easy to even write down and put into a book, except for the fact that people are forever asking me how they can make a really great dressing at home. It's all about balance and respect.

'What does that mean?' you may ask. Well, you need to respect the ingredients that you are dressing — if you are tossing a few leaves then a very light hand is required, as over-dressing will destroy the leaves and any of the delicate flavours you are trying to capture. On the other hand, if you have some particularly juicy and delicious tomatoes or a thick chunk of poached leek, then they like to be dressed generously, and then left to sit in the dressing to marinate. 'Balance' refers to the quantity of oil, vinegar and seasoning that you add to a dressing. The rough rule of thumb is one part acid (for example, vinegar, lemon or lime) and two parts oil for the base, then you can start adding salt, pepper, spices and sugar, as you see fit. Also remember that your dressing does not need to be made fresh for every meal — make a jar of the stuff and keep it in the fridge for when you want it.

My red wine dressing
Makes 200 ml (7 fl oz)

55 ml (1¾ fl oz) red wine vinegar
150 ml (5 fl oz) extra virgin olive oil
1 clove of garlic, peeled but left
  whole
salt and freshly ground black pepper

Put the vinegar, oil, garlic and seasoning in a jar and shake thoroughly. Keeps for ages. This dressing is good for just about any use and is always handy to have in the fridge.

Dahl Makhani

Serves 4–6

250 g (9 oz/1 ¼ cups) urad dahl
  (black lentils)
200 g (9 oz) tomato paste
  (concentrated purée)
500 ml (17 fl oz/2 cups) tomato
  passata (puréed tomatoes)
250 ml (9 fl oz/1 cup) pouring
  (whipping) cream, plus 1
  tablespoons extra, to serve
1 tablespoon ghee
2.5 cm (1 inch) piece of fresh
  ginger, thinly sliced
50 g (1 ¾ oz) butter

Put 1.5 litres (52 fl oz/6 cups) water in a large heavy-based saucepan and bring to the boil. Add the urad dahl and cook over medium heat for about 20 minutes, or until the grains are tender and begin to split. Add the tomato paste, tomato passata and cream and simmer (adding hot water if necessary — it should be juicy but not too wet) for at least 2 hours, or until the pulses are soft and the mixture turns a rich red colour. Remove from the heat and keep warm.

Heat the ghee in a wok or large heavy-based frying pan and sauté the ginger until the aroma has been released. Add the ginger to dahl. Stir through the butter and serve garnished with a swirl of extra cream.

Mum's corn fritters

'Open a tin of creamed corn, empty it into a bowl and add an egg, then some flour and mix it all together. Season with a bit of salt and pepper (or anything else you want), then fry dollops of the mixture in a hot frying pan with oil.' That's the corn fritter recipe that my mum would follow, but that's not how she would make them. I shall now attempt to describe the way that she would make the fritters (while trying not to do an injustice to Mum's technique).

Start your recipe by waking up on a cold, cold morning — you must be the first person awake for this recipe to really work, so it's not for the faint of heart. Turn the oven onto high heat and leave the door open, then as the kitchen starts to warm up, open the kitchen door to allow the heat to flow into the rest of the house and take the edge off the morning chill. Mix your corn fritter batter as directed above — use 1 tin of creamed corn (about 410 g/14½ oz) and mix with 1 egg and just enough plain (all-purpose) flour to form a thick batter (about 150 g/5½ oz/1 cup) — which is going to be enough to feed your sleeping, soon-to-be-hungry family (although if you need to you can easily double or triple this recipe).

Set the table, slice thick rashers of bacon, and place them into your cold frying pans with a dash of oil (use as many pans as your oven top can manage). Place over a gentle heat and fry the bacon to allow a good amount of the fat to render out, then increase the heat and keep cooking until the bacon is nice and brown. Place on a plate with baking paper, and then place the bacon in the oven and leave it in there to keep warm. Do not tip off any of the delicious bacon fat; leave it in the pans to cook your fritters in — you may need to add more oil (or lard if you have it on hand) to ensure the fritters are cooked to a delicious crispy golden. Cook the fritters in batches and place on a separate plate or platter, then add them to to the still-open oven to keep warm (secret tip here is to quietly sing or hum while cooking; if one of your children wakes up during this step, they will wake to a sound that will lighten their hearts for the rest of their life).

When you are about to cook the last batch of fritters, put the kettle on for a milky tea, open the bedroom doors, and allow the aroma of freshly cooked bacon and corn fritters to gently wake up the family!

The final step is one that I never really noticed as a hungry kid. Only as a grown-up looking back with nostalgia have I realised that Mum would not eat any breakfast until after the rest of the family had their fill.

Leek polenta with asparagus

serves 4

Polenta is often seen in restaurants and cafés in the form of a wedge or a block. What you don't realise is that when the polenta is being made the chef has gorged himself on the wonderful, creamy, soft polenta before pouring it into a pan and letting it set.

For the leek polenta
6–7 leeks
1 clove of garlic, crushed
800 ml–1 litre (28–35 fl oz) milk
100 g (3½ oz/⅔ cup) fine polenta

For the asparagus
12 spears of asparagus, trimmed
a splash of red wine dressing
  (see page 280)
a great big pinch of freshly chopped
  herbs (parsley and chives work well)

For serving
40 g (1½ oz) butter
60 g (2¼ oz/scant ⅔ cup) freshly
  grated parmesan cheese
salt and freshly ground black pepper

To make the leek polenta, first remove the roots and the green parts of the leeks, then cut the leeks lengthways and rinse them to ensure they are completely free of dirt. Chop the clean white part of the leeks into 2 cm (¾ inch) pieces — you should have about 500 g (1 lb 2 oz). Put into a saucepan with the garlic and 800 ml (28 fl oz) of the milk and cook until the leek is very soft, about 8–10 minutes of simmering.

Using a wooden spoon, vigorously stir in the polenta. Keep stirring and cooking for about 15 minutes. If your polenta starts to become too dry, add the rest of the milk — you want a nice soft polenta, like runny porridge.

About 10 minutes before you finish cooking the polenta, cook the asparagus in a saucepan of boiling salted water. You'll know the asparagus is ready when it is tender but has no crunch when you bite into it. People often cook asparagus too little, which leads to asparagus that tastes a little acidic — perfectly cooked asparagus should be delicate, sweet and only slightly al dente. Put it into a bowl with a little red wine dressing and the freshly chopped herbs.

To serve, beat the butter and most of the parmesan into your polenta. Stir vigorously, then taste for seasoning. When you are completely happy that your polenta is rich and creamy and the asparagus is tender, pour your polenta onto plates, divide up your asparagus and put it on the polenta. Splash over the dressing and the herbs from the bowl, then top with some more parmesan.

Ribollita (bread and bean soup)

Serves 4

This is a thick, hearty dish full of flavour best served to famished friends. It does require a little bit of work and a bit of planning to cook, which is why it is so important to cook more than you need as it really does taste better the next day. Just keep in mind that when you reheat it the next day it will be thicker and may require a little more liquid. It is a good idea to start with your beans and while they are cooking prepare the rest of your soup. The beans are wonderful by themselves or as a side dish for anything from barbecued lamb shoulder to steamed blue eye cod.

For the beans

150 g (5½ oz) fresh shelled borlotti (cranberry) beans (depending on the beans, you'll need 200–350 g/ 7–12 oz fresh borlotti beans in the pod. If you are using dried beans, soak 135 g/4¾ oz beans for 24 hours.)

2 overripe tomatoes

2 cloves of garlic, peeled

1 bay leaf

a few sprigs of thyme

a splash of parmesan-infused olive oil (see page 197) or extra virgin olive oil

Preheat your oven to 200°C (400°F/Gas 6). Put the beans in a casserole dish and crush the tomatoes onto the beans with your hands. Add the rest of your ingredients and cover with cold water. Do not add salt yet as it can cause the beans to become coarse and chalky when cooked. Seal your dish with a lid or wrap well with foil and bake for 1½–2 hours. Start checking the beans after 1½ hours, you want them to be delicate and tender, almost creamy in texture. If you are cooking dried beans you may need to top up with more water and cook for about twice as long. Drain, reserving the cooking liquid and fishing out the bay leaf and sprigs of thyme.

I really do hate throwing away flavour. I keep my parmesan rinds as well as any prosciutto and pancetta rinds, which is one of the reasons I love this soup — it is one of the best ways to utilise these flavoursome treasures. To store prosciutto or pancetta rinds keep them in your fridge where they can breathe; don't cover them with plastic wrap or they will sweat and go mouldy. Instead, wrap them in a piece of baking paper. I find the egg tray on the fridge door is the best spot to store them; they will sit there comfortably for a couple of weeks at least.

For the soup

2 stalks of celery

1 bulb of fennel

4 carrots, peeled

1 red onion, peeled

a small head of celeriac, peeled

2 cloves of garlic, peeled

a few sprigs of thyme, chopped

a few stalks of rosemary, leaves
only, chopped

a pinch of chilli flakes

a pinch of coriander seeds, crushed

salt and freshly ground black pepper

100 ml (3½ fl oz) extra virgin olive
oil

pancetta, prosciutto or parmesan
cheese rinds

2 litres (70 fl oz/8 cups) water or
any type of stock you have on
hand

500 g (1 lb 2 oz) tomatoes, peeled
and chopped

200 g (7 oz) cavolo nero or other
bitter green leaf, coarsely chopped

200 g (7 oz) sourdough bread, torn
(I prefer no crusts)

100 g (3½ oz) rocket (arugula),
coarsely chopped

a drizzle of parmesan-infused oil

To make the soup, coarsely chop the celery, fennel, carrots, onion, celeriac and garlic and put in a food processor with the herbs and spices. Blend until a very coarse paste forms; depending on the size of the bowl of the food processor you may need to do this in batches. Scoop into a bowl.

Since you've got the food processor out, give it quick a rinse, then blend one-third of the cooked beans with enough of the cooking liquid to form a paste and set to one side.

Heat a large heavy-based saucepan or stockpot over high heat and add the olive oil and your vegetable mix. As your mixture starts to heat, it will release its liquid; keep cooking and stirring until the mixture becomes dry and starts to give off a sweet roasted vegetable aroma. It is fine to let the mixture colour slightly but be careful not to let it stick. Now add your pancetta, prosciutto or parmesan rinds, water and tomato and bring to the boil and let simmer for 30 minutes.

Add the cavolo nero, cooked borlotti beans, bean purée and sourdough. Cook for another 15 minutes, then just before you serve your soup throw in the chopped rocket and check your seasoning — don't be shy with the salt and pepper, this soup requires a good amount. Fish out your rinds, then pour the soup into your serving bowls and add a final drizzle of your parmesan-infused oil. Serve with a wedge of bread with good butter.

Polenta cake with mushrooms, peas and rocket

Serves 4

To make a good polenta cake is dead easy. The biggest mistake that people make is to think that just because it needs to set the polenta can't have butter and cheese in it, or that it needs to be extra dry — not so. When making your polenta cake it should be as delicious and as wet as you would like to eat your soft polenta.

For preparing the polenta

1 litre (35 fl oz/4 cups) water

1 bay leaf

salt and freshly ground pepper

250 g (9 oz/1⅔ cups) polenta

125 g (4½ oz/1¼ cups) freshly grated parmesan cheese

100 g (3½ oz) diced, cold unsalted butter

vegetable oil, for cooking

For the mushroom topping

200 g (7 oz) portobello mushrooms, lower part of the stems removed, cut into quarters

200 g (7 oz) button mushrooms, cut in half

150 g (5½ oz) porcini mushrooms, cut into thick slices, or 80 g (2¾ oz) dried porcini, which have been soaked in warm water for 1 hour, then chopped

200 g (7 oz) butter

a few sprigs of thyme

2 cloves of garlic, crushed

salt and freshly ground black pepper

100 g (3½oz/1 cup) green peas, cooked

a drizzle of extra virgin olive oil

1 lemon

1 large handful of rocket (arugula)

To make the polenta, lightly grease a baking tray with a lip so it is ready for when the polenta is cooked. In a large saucepan, combine the water, bay leaf and salt and pepper and bring to a simmer. As soon as the water simmers, slowly start sprinkling in the polenta while continuously stirring with a wooden spoon. When all of the polenta has been added, keep cooking over a very gentle heat for about 20 minutes, stirring from time to time. Taste the polenta to check for doneness — it should have a slightly grainy consistency but should not be 'bitsy'.

When the polenta is ready, remove the pan from the heat, take out the bay leaf and add all of the cheese and butter and stir vigorously until everything is well incorporated. Taste this and adjust the seasoning. Pour the soft polenta into your greased baking tray and, using the back of a spoon, smooth out the polenta. Press on a piece of plastic wrap to cover the polenta and place the tray into your fridge to allow to cool completely — this will take 2–3 hours.

Preheat your oven to 190°C (375°F/Gas 5). To make the mushroom topping, combine the raw mushrooms and place onto a roasting tray that is large enough to take everything without mounding up high (a relatively thin layer will give the best results). Take your butter and cut into small dice and scatter over the mushrooms along with the sprigs of thyme and the garlic, then season. Put in your oven for 15 minutes, stir well and return to the oven for another 5–10 minutes. If you are using the dried porcini, then add to the mushrooms about halfway through the cooking. Place them into a bowl with the peas — there should be enough warmth in the mushrooms to warm the peas. Drizzle a little olive oil over the top and squeeze in a touch of lemon juice, then add the rocket and gently fold everything together.

For serving

a block of parmesan cheese

When your polenta has chilled and set, it needs to be cut into pieces and fried. The size of the pieces will depend on the shape and size of your tray. I normally cut them into 4 x 8 cm (1½ x 3¼ inch) long batons as they are easy to handle, but use your judgement to get the most out of your polenta.

Heat a large frying pan with about 5 mm (¼ inch) of vegetable oil. When the oil is nice and hot, carefully place in the polenta pieces (cook in batches if needed) and cook undisturbed for at least 5 minutes, or until you have a nice golden colour; if you handle the polenta too much, or try moving it before it has coloured properly, then it can break up and crumble. Carefully turn over the polenta and fry the other side. Lift out of the pan and drain on paper towel before transferring to your platter.

Scatter the roasted mushroom mixture over the pieces of polenta, then, using a vegetable peeler, shave over a good amount of parmesan cheese. Serve as soon as you can.

The main thing to remember when cooking polenta is not to be stingy with how much oil you use; in fact, you want the oil to come at least halfway up the polenta cake. In this recipe I have pan-fried the polenta, but if you have a deep-frier, you can cook the polenta cake that way. Don't worry too much about your polenta cake tasting oily or greasy; it won't be if your oil is at the correct temperature. There are a couple of ways to check the temperature of your oil; the most accurate is with a thermometer but you can also use the handle of a wooden spoon by dipping it in and seeing if bubbles come off it. Or, there is my favourite way — if you take a cube of white bread, drop it into your oil and it takes approximately 45 seconds to go a deep golden brown, then your oil is at 175°C (350°F).

White onion risotto with crispy pancetta and parsley oil

Serves 4

You can change the stock if you want a different flavour in this risotto, but keep the technique the same for all your risottos. Every chef has a slightly different way of doing risotto, but for me this is it. Rue the day someone comes into my kitchen with some fancy pants effortless way of cooking risotto.

For the onion stock
750 g (1 lb 10 oz) white onions
(these are sweeter and juicier than
brown onions and work best for
this recipe)
2 tablespoons oil
½ teaspoon salt
1.25 litres (44 fl oz/5 cups) water

For the parsley oil
1 bunch of flat-leaf (Italian) parsley,
chopped
100 ml (3½ fl oz) extra virgin olive
oil
a pinch of salt

For the crispy pancetta
100 g (3½ oz) long, thin slices of
pancetta

To make the onion stock, thinly slice the onions and place in a cold saucepan with the oil and salt. Add a tight-fitting lid and place over medium–low heat. When you start to get heat through your onions, stir from time to time to ensure that they do not colour — very important! Keep the lid on your saucepan as much as possible; what will happen is that the steam will start to build up and gently pull all of the super sweet onion juices out of the onions. When the onions have become soft, 12 minutes or so, cover with cold water, bring to the boil and simmer for no longer than 5 minutes. Purée this onion stock in a blender, then pass through a fine sieve. The stock can be made in advance and stored in the fridge until you need it.

To make the parsley oil, put all the ingredients in a blender or food processor and purée until a paste forms. Set aside.

Preheat your oven to 200°C (400°F/Gas 6). To make the crispy pancetta, put thin slices of pancetta on baking paper and cook in the oven until crispy (4–5 minutes), then drain on crumpled paper towels before letting cool on a wire rack.

For the risotto

40 g (1½ oz) butter

1 white onion, finely diced

2 cloves of garlic, finely chopped

220 g (7¾ oz/1 cup) arborio rice

a handful of freshly grated
parmesan cheese

an extra knob (or as much as you
want) of good butter to finish
the rice

This recipe makes
more parsley oil
than you'll need for
the risotto, but it will keep
for a couple of weeks in a
sterilised jar in the fridge and
it is great brushed over grilled
(broiled) meat or fish or used
in dressings. Bring to room
temperature before using.

To make the risotto, melt the butter in a heavy-based saucepan over medium heat, then add the onion and garlic. Keep stirring and do not let colour — when the onion has become soft and sweet turn up the heat, add the rice and stir vigorously. You want to keep stirring the rice over the heat for about 10 minutes — this will improve the flavour of your risotto, also it prepares the rice well for absorbing all that stock and flavour without the grains 'bursting' and looking crumbly.

Have your hot onion stock near at hand and start adding the stock, one ladle at a time, waiting until it is all absorbed before adding the next ladle. During the process you keep stirring, stirring, stirring — a sure sign of a good risotto is an aching arm and little beads of sweat on your forehead. Your rice is cooked when it is tender but not chalky in the middle, this may or may not involve all of your onion stock, and you may even have to add a little extra stock or water. I like to let the rice sit for a couple of minutes before finishing (just enough time to pour some wine and allow your arm to rest before the final effort).

Stir almost all of your cheese and as much butter as you want into the risotto and beat until all is well incorporated and creamy — adjust the consistency with a touch more stock or water if needed. Risotto must be soft and beautiful and slide into your mouth; if it is dry and crumbly it is forgettable and hard to eat.

To serve, pour your finished risotto onto plates or a platter and drizzle with as much of the parsley oil as you want. Layer the pancetta over the top and sprinkle with cheese.

Spaghetti with cauliflower strascicata

Serves 4

At first glance it looks like there is way too much chopping in this recipe and the fried cauliflower may seem strange to some people. But as soon as you start cooking and all of the aromas come together, you'll find it very difficult not to start eating it straight out of the pan — the bits stuck to the bottom of the pan are best eaten in greedy solitude.

400 g (14 oz) spaghetti

100 ml (3½ fl oz) extra virgin olive oil

½ head of cauliflower, chopped into pieces about the size of your thumbnail

3 cloves of garlic, thinly sliced

3 anchovy fillets, chopped

2 large red chillies, chopped (keep the seeds in if you like things hot)

50 g (1¾ oz) salted capers, rinsed and chopped

100 g (3½ oz) pitted olives, chopped

1 bunch of flat-leaf (Italian) parsley, chopped

60 g (2¼ oz) toasted sourdough breadcrumbs (see page 297)

200 g (7 oz/2 cups) freshly grated parmesan cheese

1 lemon, cut into wedges

Cook the spaghetti in a large pot of boiling water until al dente. Drain, then cool; while cooling drizzle with a little of the oil, then gently toss.

In a large heavy-based frying pan heat the rest of the oil over medium heat, add the cauliflower and fry until just starting to colour. Add the garlic, mix well, then add the anchovies, chilli, capers and olives. When the cauliflower starts to become tender and has a rich golden colour, add half of the parsley and the cooked spaghetti. When the pasta is hot, add the breadcrumbs, parmesan and remainder of the parsley.

The parmesan will start to stick to the pan; use a wooden spoon to scrape the bottom of the pan (this is where the term strascicata comes from, meaning drag). Remove from the heat and serve immediately with a wedge of lemon.

Lyonnaise sausage and lentil stew

Serves 4

For this dish I like to use a lyonnaise sausage, which is a peppery pork sausage that is warming and rich. I get them made by a mate of mine who forms the sausage meat into a beef casing called a 'bung'. This is a large piece of intestine that stops in a dead end. When cleaned, salted, rinsed and stuffed it makes a sausage that is around 12 cm (4½ inches) in diameter and 50 cm (20 inches) long and weighs around 1.5 kg (3 lb 5 oz). I like to be able to serve a big fat disc of sausage topped with a runny poached egg. You may not be able to get a sausage the size I have just described; however, any good pork sausages will do just as well.

For the stew

600–800 g (1 lb 5 oz–1 lb 12 oz) lyonnaise sausage or other pork sausages

2 carrots, peeled and sliced

2 bay leaves

a knob of butter

1 onion, diced

1 clove of garlic, crushed

½ teaspoon fennel seeds

½ teaspoon ground white pepper

185 g (6½ oz/1 cup) puy lentils or tiny blue–green lentils

400 g (14 oz) tin peeled tomatoes, broken up a little, juice and all

Put the lyonnaise sausage or pork sausages in a saucepan with just enough cold water to cover, then add the carrot and bay leaves and bring to a simmer and gently poach. The time you need depends on the size of the sausage(s) — you can test by poking the meat with your finger, it should be nice and firm. Take the pan off the heat. Allow the sausage(s) to cool in the liquid. When cool, remove the sausage(s) and peel off the skin. If you are using a lyonnaise sausage cut it into thick discs; if you are using normal sausages, cut into thick pieces. Reserve the cooking liquid (you won't use the carrot or bay leaves, though).

In a clean saucepan over high heat, soften a little butter and fry the sausage pieces until they are nice and brown. Remove the sausage pieces and add the onion, garlic, fennel and pepper. Cook until soft, then add the lentils, tomato, 500 ml (17 fl oz/2 cups) of the sausage cooking liquid (don't throw out the rest) and the browned pieces of sausage. The lentils will take around 30 minutes of cooking to get them nice and tender — a little overcooked doesn't matter too much but be sure not to serve any firm lentils. If the lentils look like they need more liquid, add some more of the sausage cooking liquid or water.

When you are ready to serve, taste your stew — I like mine to have a warm white pepper flavour, which will be balanced out with a runny poached egg yolk.

Melba toasts

Makes 32

8 slices of white bread

Preheat your oven to 170°C (325°F/Gas 3). Lightly toast one side of the bread under the grill (broiler). Allow to cool, then cut off the crust while trying to keep your piece of bread as square as possible. Using a large sharp knife, carefully split the bread through the middle so that you end up with two pieces of bread with one side toasted and the other side being soft bread. Cut each piece into four triangles.

Now comes the fun part. You want to 'rub' the soft bread off the toasted bread — you can do this by placing one of the little triangles on your chopping board, toasted side up, then press the palm of your hand down on the bread quite firmly and start to make little circles. After a couple of moments you should end up with a wafer-thin slice of toasted bread; don't panic if there is still a little of the bread on the toast.

Once you have rubbed all of your bread, place the triangles onto a baking tray, toasted side up, and then into the oven for 5–6 minutes until they curl up slightly and go a crispy golden brown. Once they have cooled they will be very fragile so be careful how you handle them, as nothing is as annoying as breaking all of your toasts before you get to show them off.

Breadcrumbs

Making your own breadcrumbs is easier if you use bread that is a day or two old, but you can use fresh bread to make fresh breadcrumbs. Simply place your bread in a blender or food processor and blend well until powdered. Shake your crumbs through a coarse sieve to remove larger pieces of crumb.

To make toasted breadcrumbs, spread a layer of crumbs (you don't need to sieve them) on a baking tray and bake in a preheated 160°C (315°F/Gas 2–3) oven until a nice gold colour, stirring often ot make sure the colour is even.

To make herbed breadcrumbs, add some chopped herbs and/or a clove of garlic to the blender. Heat a drizzle of olive oil and a large knob of butter in a large frying pan and cook breadcrumbs until well coloured, then drain on paper towels before using.

Baba Gewürztraminer

Serves 6

Typically, a baba is soaked in a syrup made from dark rum. I came up with this version one night when trying to pair a dessert with a particularly delicious Gewürztraminer. I really like the results as this wine variety is big enough in flavour and body to enable some very good flavour combinations. It is best to make the syrup first.

For the syrup

150 ml (5 fl oz) water

335 g (11¾ oz/1½ cups) sugar

6 dried apricots

6 pieces of dried pear

1 vanilla bean, split

400 ml (14 fl oz) Gewürztraminer wine

For the babas

60 g (2¼ oz/½ cup) raisins

100 ml (3½ fl oz) Gewürztraminer wine

1 teaspoon dried yeast

80 ml (2½ fl oz/⅓ cup) milk, warmed slightly

125 g (4½ oz/1 cup) plain (all-purpose) flour

2 eggs

a big pinch of sugar

a pinch of salt

100 g (3½ oz) unsalted butter, softened

To make the syrup, combine the water and sugar in a saucepan, then place over a high heat and stir until the sugar has dissolved, then add the dried fruit, vanilla bean and wine. Bring back up to heat but do not boil. Just before it is about to simmer, remove from the heat and allow to cool.

To make the babas, put the raisins in a small bowl with the wine and set to one side to soak. In a large bowl, dissolve the yeast in the milk and let it sit for a moment. Now mix in the flour and eggs and beat until you have a smooth dough, then cover with plastic wrap and allow to prove at room temperature for about 45 minutes.

Preheat your oven to 180°C (350°F/Gas 4). Add the sugar, salt and butter to the batter, mixing vigorously to incorporate. When all of the butter is combined, add the soaked raisins and wine and beat really well again.

Grease a six-hole 125 ml (4 fl oz/½ cup) muffin tin with a little butter before dividing the batter among the holes. Let the mixture rise until the holes are full, then place them in the oven for 20–25 minutes until golden. To test if the babas are ready, insert a skewer and if it comes out clean the babas are cooked.

When the babas have been allowed to cool slightly, lift them from the tin, place them into the syrup and let them soak for at least 20 minutes. You can actually store the babas in the syrup overnight. When you are ready to serve, lift a baba onto a plate and add a piece of the apricot and pear. Spoon some of the syrup into a saucepan and place over high heat and bring to the boil. Pour the hot syrup over the cake and if you feel inclined, serve with a little whipped cream.

Eccles cakes

This recipe is similar to the ones originally baked in Church Street in Eccles, Manchester. Eccles cakes are typically made from currants that have been steeped in water, then mixed with butter and sugar. I prefer the results you get from cooking muscatel grapes to get their sugar going. These are great on their own but my absolute favourite way of serving them is to serve them at room temperature next to a wheel of ripe cheese.

120 g (4¼ oz) unsalted butter

335 g (11¾ oz) dried muscatel grapes, picked off the stem, or raisins

135 g (4¾ oz/scant ⅔ cup) caster (superfine) sugar, plus extra, for sprinkling

grated zest of most of a lemon

juice of 1½ lemons

about 8 sheets of bought puff pastry (the number of sheets you need will depend on the size of your pastry sheets)

1 egg, lightly beaten

Melt the butter in a saucepan. Add the grapes, sugar, lemon zest and juice and cook everything over a medium heat until the muscatels start to puff up and the sugars start to caramelize, about 10 minutes. Remove the pan from the heat and allow to cool completely — this will take at least 2 hours.

Preheat your oven to 180°C (350°F/Gas 4) and grease a baking tray. Cut 24 x 10 cm (4 inch) discs from the puff pastry — you can use a saucer as a guide. Place a small dollop of fruit into the middle of each disc (using up all the fruit mixture), then brush the edges of the pastry with the egg. Pick up each disc and pull the edges into the middle of the fruit until you have completely covered the fruit and sealed the parcels. Place them on the baking tray, seam side down. Use a very sharp knife to score the top of the cakes. Brush with the egg and sprinkle with caster sugar.

Bake for 10–12 minutes, then sprinkle with a little more sugar and bake for a further 5–10 minutes. Don't worry if a couple of the cakes explode. When they are completely cooked and well coloured remove them from the oven. There will be some sticky juice that has oozed out during the cooking; carefully roll the cakes in that sticky ooze while it is still hot, then transfer the cakes to a wire rack.

Grown-up hot chocolate

Serves 8

600 ml (21 fl oz) milk

400 ml (14 fl oz) pouring (whipping) cream

1 bird's eye chilli

1 star anise

1 piece of cinnamon

2 green cardamom pods, crushed

a pinch of salt

110 g (3¾ oz/scant 1 cup) unsweetened cocoa powder

350 g (12 oz) good-quality chocolate melts (buttons) (see note page 27)

80 g (2¾ oz) bittersweet chocolate, grated

185 ml (6 fl oz/¾ cup) crème de cacao

30 ml (1 fl oz) Bacardi (white rum)

30 ml (1 fl oz) orange juice

Start by combining the milk and cream in a saucepan with your spices and salt. Place this on a very gentle heat and allow to slowly come up to a simmer, stirring from time to time. Allow this mixture to simmer for another 10 minutes to get as much infused flavour from your spices. Strain.

Place the cocoa into a clean saucepan and add the strained infused milk and cream mixture a little at a time; keep whisking to ensure that there are no lumps. Once all of the milk has been incorporated, add the chocolate buttons and the grated chocolate and whisk well until everything is melted and combined. If you are serving straight away, add the crème de cacao, Bacardi and orange juice and stir well.

If you are not going to serve your hot chocolate straight away, set the mixture aside; alternatively, this can be stored in the fridge and kept for the next day (blended with ice it will make a particularly good chocolate milkshake). When you come to reheat your hot chocolate, place the mixture onto a gentle heat and stir often, without letting the chocolate come to the boil. When you are just about to serve, add the crème de cacao, Bacardi and orange juice and stir thoroughly. Serve immediately.

The best chocolate cake recipe I know

Serves 16

This cake has all of the bases covered — it is chocolate, it is rich, it is fabulous! But there is a catch. It cannot be eaten on the same day it is made; you must show a little restraint when making it. The other small catch is that you must use really good chocolate. I am not being a food snob (I'll be the first one to crave a dodgy chocolate bar after a great meal), but the simple reality is that cooking chocolate or white chocolate will not work — trust me on this as I have tried (in vain) to short-cut this recipe and it is not the same.

butter, for greasing
plain (all-purpose) flour, for dusting
500 g (1 lb 2 oz) good-quality dark
  chocolate, chopped (see note)
250 g (9 oz) unsalted butter,
  chopped
10 eggs
a pinch of salt
50 g (1¾ oz/¼ cup) caster
  (superfine) sugar
35 g (1¼ oz/¼ cup) plain
  (all-purpose) flour

As with all chocolate recipes, it is well worth the effort seeking out the best quality good-quality chocolate you can find. My preference is to use Callebaut '811' chocolate with around 53% cocoa solids. It is available from most speciality grocery stores.

Preheat your oven to 205°C (400°F/Gas 6). Now prepare a 22 cm (8½ inch) spring-form cake tin by rubbing with a little butter and dusting with flour. Have ready a lightly greased (but not floured) flat ovenproof dinner plate that will be large enough to sit over the edges of your tin.

Put the chocolate and butter in a clean heatproof bowl, then place the bowl over a saucepan of simmering water, without letting the base of the bowl touch the water. Gently melt the chocolate. While this is happening, start to carefully separate your eggs, placing the yolks in one small bowl and the whites into a large bowl or the bowl of an electric mixer with a whisking attachment (if you prefer, you can whisk the whites by hand using a balloon whisk and brute force, but an electric mixer will make the job much easier).

When the chocolate and butter have melted, add a pinch of salt, stir well and remove from the heat to allow it to cool slightly. While this is happening, start to whisk your egg whites. When your egg whites have formed soft peaks, sprinkle in the sugar and continue to whisk for about 1 more minute, or until the sugar has dissolved and the whites take on a nice shine. Now add the flour to the egg yolks and mix thoroughly.

The cooking times and temperatures for this cake are quite precise and worth following the first time, but you will probably find that the second time you make this recipe it will be better, as you will be able to make little changes to the times and temperature to suit your own oven.

You now need a clean large bowl in which to mix everything. Start by pouring in your melted chocolate mixture, then, using a whisk, beat in your egg yolk and flour mixture really well. Now, using your hands, fold your egg white mixture into the chocolate, one-third at a time, being careful to combine everything, but do not overwork. Working quickly, pour the chocolate batter into your prepared tin, then place into the oven for 15 minutes. After 15 minutes gently place the prepared plate, greased side down, on top of the cake tin (by now the cake will have started to rise) and put the tin back into the oven for 12 minutes. Once the cooking time has finished, resist the urge to lift the plate (but if you do and the cake looks unset and runny, don't panic, this is what it is supposed to look like) and place the cake (still in its tin, covered by the plate) on a wire rack out of direct sunlight, in a cool spot for at least 24 hours.

The next day carefully lift off the dinner plate. You will find that the cake will have sunk in the middle and will look a little ugly, but do not judge a book by its cover because you are about to have a wonderful chocolate experience. Carefully unclip and remove the side of the spring-form tin. Use a knife that has been heated in hot water and then dried to cut slices of your cake and simply serve with fresh tart berries and cream. Your cake should have the texture of a smooth and exotic pâté. Do not place the cake in the fridge as it will sit at room temperature for about 2 days. Enjoy.

Acknowledgements

Writing is one of those weird jobs – when things are flowing you almost feel guilty calling it a job! It's easy, fun, bloody beautiful – life simply doesn't get much better! Then there are those time when it is not – it's really hard and nothing flows. It's times like that an author (me) feels such a huge and unwavering appreciation for a great publisher (Murdoch Books).

This book would simply not exist if Kay Scarlett had not had called me up with 'an interesting project' and Jane Lawson was right there with huge encouragement. However once begun, projects like this one tend to develop a life of their own. Here are my "Jared... we go to go to print tomorrow" observations.

I've been lucky enough to have Livia Caiazzo, Jacqueline Blanchard, Tania Gomes and Joan Beal lend their talents to this book and get it to where it is today. Alan Benson and his ability to take a great pic has added a flavour that only he can and stylists Jane Hann, Mary Harris and Margot Braddon all made it an awesome shoot!

Thanks to Danks Street Depot and to all of those that have been a part of that remarkable story. There are far too many people to mention but this book would not exist without the thousands of back breaking hours of work undertaken by a collection of the best damn looking bunch of cooks, waiters, runners, kitchen hands, PR peeps, PAs along with behind-the-scenes legend Tony Cranes (congrats on the new family!)

Arkin and 'Lampo' – thanks for your help boys.

To 'the iron fist in the velvet glove', Kylie Walker, this book would not be here without you. Seriously, this was a tough gig (this book was written twice, I opened a new restaurant Cotton Duck and just about anything that could have gone wrong did... more than once) and yet you never lost faith in this project. I'm very proud of what has been achieved and I'm so very thankful for your efforts!

Finally, a big thanks to all the farmers, producers, providores, butchers, fishmongers, bakers, cheesemakers, cooks and the consumers who understand the beauty of food and the importance of diversity and respect. Thanks also to Slow food and Carlo Petrini – Terra Madre was a very important moment in my life! I was one of a thousand cooks, a face in the crowd, caught up in a love affair with a romantic ideology based on commonsense and beauty. The brief conversation about food and politics we had at BirdCowFish in Sydney gave me the fortitude to continue to celebrate food and when needed, fight for Mother Nature!

Eat Well,

Jared Ingersoll

Published in 2011 by Murdoch Books Pty Limited

Murdoch Books Australia
Pier 8/9
23 Hickson Road
Millers Point NSW 2000
Phone: +61 (0) 2 8220 2000
Fax: +61 (0) 2 8220 2558
www.murdochbooks.com.au

Murdoch Books UK Limited
Erico House, 6th Floor
93–99 Upper Richmond Road
Putney, London SW15 2TG
Phone: +44 (0) 20 8785 5995
Fax: +44 (0) 20 8785 5985
www.murdochbooks.co.uk

Publisher: Kylie Walker
Designer: Tania Gomes
Photographer: Alan Benson
Stylists: Jane Hann, Margot Braddon, Mary Harris
Project Manager: Livia Caiazzo
Editor: Jacqueline Blanchard
Production Controller: Joan Beal

National Library of Australia Cataloguing-in-Publication entry
Author: Ingersoll, Jared.
Title: Slow food : a passion for produce / Jared Ingersoll.
ISBN: 9781741969252 (pbk.)
Notes: Includes index.
Subjects: Cooking.
Dewey Number: 641.5

A catalogue record for this book is available from the British Library.

Printed by 1010 Printing International Limited, China

IMPORTANT: Those who might be at risk from the effects of salmonella poisoning (the elderly, pregnant
women, young children and those suffering from immune deficiency diseases) should consult their doctor
with any concerns about eating raw eggs.

OVEN GUIDE: You may find cooking times vary depending on the oven you are using. For fan-forced ovens,
as a general rule, set the oven temperature to 20°C (35°F) lower than indicated in the recipe.